OVERCOMING
ADVERSITY

KEVIN LaChapelle

OVERCOMING ADVERSITY

iUniverse books may be ordered through booksellers or by contacting:

iUniverse
1663 Liberty Drive
Bloomington, IN 47403
www.iuniverse.com
1-800-Authors (1-800-288-4677)

Because of the dynamic nature of the Internet, any web addresses or links contained in this book may have changed since publication and may no longer be valid. The views expressed in this work are solely those of the author and do not necessarily reflect the views of the publisher, and the publisher hereby disclaims any responsibility for them.

Any people depicted in stock imagery provided by Thinkstock are models, and such images are being used for illustrative purposes only. Certain stock imagery © Thinkstock.

ISBN: 978-1-4917-5913-4 (sc)
ISBN: 978-1-4917-5914-1 (hc)
ISBN: 978-1-4917-5912-7 (e)

Library of Congress Control Number: 2015903550

Print information available on the last page.

iUniverse rev. date: 3/26/2015

CONTENTS

Foreword vii

Preface xi

Chapter 1   The New Protégé 1

Chapter 2   Others Have Done It, and So Can You. 19

Chapter 3   Nothing Is Impossible 57

Chapter 4   Mentoring Doesn't Stop With You. 81

Chapter 5   Mentees Learning to Mentor Others 91

Chapter 6   Letting Go. 98

Chapter 7   Lessons in Leadership 109

Chapter 8   Your Future Awaits You 158

Foreword

In February 1997, my father was missing, and instead of helping with the search, local law enforcement chalked it up to a domestic dispute and brushed us off. During this time, we were introduced to Kevin LaChapelle over lunch at a small restaurant in Pacific Beach, California. Drawing on his law-enforcement experience and connections with local authorities, he volunteered to spearhead the search for my father. Kevin and his team found my father in the Sierra Mountains, where he had been hiking, slipped down a ravine, and ultimately perished. While this search did not have a happy ending, one of the blessings that did come out of those trying times was my lifelong friendship with Kevin.

The loss of my father was one of the defining moments of my adolescence. It had the potential to start a downward spiral in my life. While a father is irreplaceable, the loss or absence of one doesn't necessarily have to start a cycle of personal decline. By God's Providence, He placed extraordinary people in the form of high school football coaches, teachers, and others like Kevin in my life who were able and ready to fill in for the leadership, discipline, and mentorship my father had provided.

In today's American society, the breakdown of the family unit and absence of two parents (especially fathers) in our children's lives is the most often overlooked and ignored social crisis. In my opinion, it is the largest causal effect of our current societal problems. One can choose nearly any social statistic (propensity for drug abuse, suicide rates, inclination toward violent crime, graduation rates, income inequality, etc.) and find that children from single-parent homes are at a disadvantage across all of them. Depending on the study cited, over the past decade, approximately 32 percent to 40 percent of American children are being raised in single-parent homes. While the majority of single-family homes are a result of having children outside of marriage, a large subset is due to divorce. Death of a spouse or single-parent adoption account for a very small percentage of single-parent homes.

This rate is even more pronounced in minority communities, where, in 2013, 70 percent of African Americans and 50 percent of Latino Americans were born to single mothers. Additionally, the vast majority of these single-parent families are from poor or middle-class income brackets. It is easy to see that these children are growing up in an environment where all the odds are stacked against them, starting at birth.

Well understood are the economic disadvantages of single-parent homes, as it is easy to ascertain that two incomes are better than one. However, less often stated, yet more important, is the loss of the second parent's time and influence. On the subject of time, it is very difficult for a single parent, especially one having to work extra to make up for lost income, to spend the same amount of quality time that a two-parent home would be able to spend with their children. This loss of quality time is detrimental to a child's development. Quality time is what it takes for a mentor to instill in a child the traits of moral character, emotional intelligence, and work ethic. In short, not having a second parent deprives the child of a second primary source of attention, ideas, guidance, discipline, and perspective (just to name a few). In my opinion, this is even more detrimental than the lack of income and resources. Even a child with few resources and a plentiful amount of positive influence and mentorship still has a very good chance of being a productive member of society. Nearly 40 percent of an entire American generation, through no fault of their own, are growing up deprived of this second source of parental guidance and mentorship. The breakdown of the two-parent home is creating a need for mentorship of the younger generations on a scale that the United States has never seen before.

While nothing can fully replace an active parent, a mentor can help to fill the gap and encourage the development of an individual to reach that person's full potential. The impact of mentors is often understated, but many of history's most powerful and influential people were profoundly impacted by an active mentor. In ancient times, one of the most successful emperors and military commanders was Alexander the Great. By the age of thirty, he had created one of the largest empires the world had seen up to that point. Unfortunately, what most people don't know is that until the age of sixteen, he was tutored by Aristotle, one of the most famous and influential philosophers and intellectuals in history. This tutoring unlocked the potential in Alexander, and his subsequent conquests spread Greek culture to the world. Many aspects of Ancient Greek culture are the foundation for today's modern thought.

In modern times, we sing the praises of Martin Luther King Jr. We even have a national holiday to celebrate the work he did in advancing the cause of civil rights through peaceful protest. But what many do not know is that Benjamin Mays, the president of Morehouse College, was the primary influence upon a whole generation of African American preachers, most notably Martin Luther King, whom he took a personal interest in. While King may have been the leader and primary voice of the civil rights movement in the 1960s, its philosophical and ideological roots were sourced from Benjamin May. Benjamin May himself was also profoundly impacted by mentorship. At the urging of Howard Thurman, Benjamin May spent a lot of time in India speaking with Mahatma Gandhi. Those conversations were the genesis of the nonviolent, peaceful protest philosophy so prevalent in the civil rights movement. Reverend May found that it complemented perfectly his idea of Christian love, and he wove it into his social and political strategy. It is not a stretch to say that Mahatma Gandhi and Benjamin May were the intellectual and philosophical grandfather and father of the civil rights movement here in America.

As the examples cited above, the story you are about to read demonstrates the profound impact that mentorship can have upon the mentor, the mentee, and, subsequently, on society at large. It's a story of one man's personal commitment to develop members of a younger generation to achieve their highest potential and, in turn, realize that he himself had much more potential than he thought possible. For, at the end of the day, mentorship is about the exchange of ideas, knowledge, and wisdom from one person to another. These things are more important than any currency or resource because they have a rate of return no currency can match. Two people can exchange a dollar, but at the end of the day, they will each only have one dollar. But if two people exchange a good idea, they will each have two good ideas. Knowledge and wisdom passed down from generation to generation have an accumulating effect, and for the first time in modern history, we are in danger of losing that effect in the basic unit of our society—the family. My hope and prayer is that those reading this book, both young and old, would be influenced to take action and both seek out someone to mentor and seek out someone to be mentored by. The mentorship relationship can be one of the most rewarding relationships for an individual, and I hope you, the reader, will come to know this through your own experiences.

I have been a personal witness and beneficiary of mentorship from the people in this story. It is a story that needs to be told, and I hope that one day each of you will get to tell similar stories of the people in your lives whom you were mentored by and others in whom you were able to invest your time, knowledge, and resources—people who could look at you and say they wouldn't be the people they are without your influence in their lives. The need in our society is greater than it has ever been. Will you answer the call?

Aaron Hollenberg earned his bachelor's in computer science at the University of San Diego and a master's of business administration at New York University. Aaron currently works for Google.

Preface

It has been a privilege to witness the amazing transformations I have seen over the years, all of which have, in turn, transformed my life as I grow and mature. My source of happiness is being part of the growth and development in others and drawing out their potential and their ability to reach their dreams and goals. That happiness culminated in the founding of PowerMentor, an organization committed to developing future leaders, one person at a time. After leaving law enforcement in 1995, it was important to continue the work that I had developed while working as a police officer with inner-city Latino gangs. I also have fulfillment in the transformation of my life, resulting from their impact on me, as well as the impact my life has had on those I have had the opportunity to mentor. As you will see in the pages to follow, who we were is not nearly as important as who we become.

The true stories found in this book have inspired many young people to do the same and make changes for the betterment of their lives, allowing them to reach goals they never thought possible. The lives of each person in this book continue to thrive as they each continually impact their world though their influence and example to beat the odds! The amazing individuals you will soon read about serve as my purpose in writing this book. A tribute to their tenacity, this book offers insight into what occurred behind the scenes to activate the lives of many who were stagnant and change them to lives filled with purpose and vision.

CHAPTER ONE
The New Protégé

In 1998, while waiting for my order at a drive-through in the inner city of San Diego, California, I felt the need to encourage the seventeen-year-old drive-through attendant. I only asked him if he planned on attending college. The neighborhood indicated that the attendant was more than likely the recipient of a tough life in this inner-city area known for high gang activity and crime.

Jose Orozco, head shaven, shared that he had dropped out of high school and figured that if he worked hard, he could one day become a shift leader at the fast-food restaurant. I asked him to reflect on when he was younger—what had he dreamt of becoming? He broke away from his serious and intense demeanor and smiled, saying that he wanted to be a lawyer. I told him that he could whatever he set your mind to.

After seeing this same young man a few times at this restaurant, with my background in law-enforcement gang intervention, I felt compelled to assert myself to dig deeper and see if Jose was seeking a better life. I brought him a GED packet so he could finish school and go to college. I gave him my business card and assured him that I believed in him. I told him if he was serious, I would help him go to college.

After getting to know Jose for a few months, Jose began sharing with me the challenges of his life, such as how he had been on his own for many years after his mother had died when he was only eight years old and his father died when he was twelve, both of cancer. Jose also did not have legal status in the United States.

What would transpire over the next fifteen years is something that we only see in movies, yet this was real life. Jose earned his GED, attended junior college, and then went to San Diego State University, where he earned a double bachelor's degree in philosophy and political science. During this time, Jose received his Certificate of Citizenship. He was then accepted to law school, graduated, and is now a practicing attorney! Amazing, right?

Here is where it gets even more amazing. During this journey, Jose would ask me why I never went to college, as I was encouraging everyone else to do just that. I explained that I barely made it out of high school and had ADHD and that I was not cut out for college. I explained that when I became a police officer, I had only a high school diploma. I would share the challenges of working as a police officer with ADHD. Jose did not accept that and told me that I was making excuses and should enroll in college. He and I started college at the same time, and we did homework together every weekend.

Attending college was extremely difficult for both Jose and me. We would find ourselves encouraging each other as we met weekly to help each other with homework. Jose was great at math, while he struggled with writing. I, on the other hand, struggled with math yet had strong writing skills. Where Jose was weak, I was strong and vice versa.

At times, Jose would reflect and wonder whether all of this commitment to college would one day pay off. Jose was very worried about obtaining his legal documentation in the United States. Because of his doubt, it would cause him to feel helpless. I encouraged him, saying I firmly believed that he would reap what he sowed. He, in turn, encouraged me, saying that my working hard for a college degree would pay off for me as well. This iron-sharpening-iron friendship would keep us on track and moving forward.

During this time, Jose would become acquainted with another young man a few years younger, Agustin Peña. He would do for Agustin what I did for him. Agustin also enrolled in junior college, then San Diego State University, and then law school. While Agustin was at San Diego State University, his fourteen-year-old brother was shot and killed during a random act of violence. Agustin pressed on, knowing that the greatest gift he could give to his little brother was to live his life for both of them. Agustin is now a practicing attorney!

During Agustin's journey, he met a young man named Irving Pedroza. He walked alongside Irving, and now Irving has graduated law school, and he too is now a practicing attorney!

During Irving's journey, yet another young man came along named Jose Olivera. Irving walked alongside him, and he is currently in law school. Jose, now fired up, met a young man named Luis Gonzalez who was also in law school, and they both walked side by side through their journey.

As for my own journey through college, while Jose earned his bachelor's degree, I earned mine. While Jose attended law school, I earned my master's degree. While Agustin attended law school, I earned my doctorate. All of this did not come easily. In fact, those were some of the most challenging times of my life. ADHD would rear its ugly head every day as I tried to study and stay focused. As I would see the guys I was mentoring progress in their lives, I felt compelled that I too must progress as a matter of principle. Many times I felt like giving up; however, that was not an option.

I recall proofreading papers for the guys, and over the years, I could see major progress in their writing skills. In my life, I began to see progress in my reasoning skills, my ability to see things that I had never seen before. For example, things I learned in college, I applied in the workplace, and this theory and practice working collectively helped me recognize that I was most certainly developing my leadership skills, emotional intelligence, and overall sense of responsibility.

As I progressed through each degree, I saw progress in the form of job opportunities that I once did not see possible. For example, prior to attending college, I worked as a police officer. I was then asked to run for a local school board race, which I won. In my role as a police officer and school board member, I did not possess the skills that I discovered college would afford me.

After I earned my bachelor's degree, an opportunity opened up for me to oversee training and organizational development for the Hotel Del Coronado. This was amazing, as I would begin to see talent from within that I had not seen before. After earning my master's degree, I would be recruited for a leadership position in health care. I would never have thought that I would one day be working in health care. After earning my doctorate, I would find doors opening for the expertise I had developed in mentoring people who are a part of Generation Y, whom many organizations find are a challenge.

All of this started with the power of an encouraging word. Even though we were all told at one point by others and ourselves that we did not have what it takes to accomplish our dreams, we found someone who saw something in each of us that others did not see. Not only were Jose and Agustin impacted, but my life was also forever changed.

As all of the others were impacted, we chose to impact someone else through encouraging words and walking alongside each other, at times, believing in the other more than we believed in ourselves.

Interestingly, Jose is a deputy public defender, while Agustin is a deputy district attorney, and occasionally they meet to face one another in court. When they appeared in one such court, the judge had a recollection of them. Before he was a judge, he had been an attorney and met young Jose who was working toward earning his GED.

It is remarkable that Jose would be drawn to a position to advocate for others. He had been afforded the same benefit when he needed his legal status in the United States changed. I can remember times when Jose would be brought to tears after we received notification from immigration that additional paperwork was required for his status to become legal. Jose would see firsthand the power that comes from advocating for others. Agustin would be drawn to standing up for victims through his role as a prosecutor. He knew something about being a victim because of the senseless killing of his little brother.

— — —

As I reflect back on my first meeting with Jose at that fast-food restaurant, the success and struggle we all have experienced since 1998 makes me shake my head in wonder. How strange and beautiful life can be, just as it can be full of pain and travail. Flashing forward to 2014, I now find myself engaged in another budding relationship with my newest protégé. Interestingly enough, I met him in a restaurant, just like I'd met Jose so many years ago.

"Good morning, sir. My name is Anthony. How may I help you today?"

A young Hispanic, possibly in his early twenties, seemed eager to greet me. He was a slender-looking man, rough around the edges. Yet, his smile was inviting and welcoming. It led me to believe there was something great about him beneath his unpolished exterior.

My stomach was rumbling, and I was ready to quickly place my order. "I would like to order a six-cheese bagel, please."

On a Monday morning, I can't think of a better way to start my week off than with a fresh-baked gourmet bagel from Einstein Bros Bagels. I've been known to come to the company's La Jolla location from time to time. Because their bagels are always fresh and their employees are quick and efficient, it's the perfect pit stop before I head to work.

I had been employed at Scripps Health for about four years, starting in 2008. Mainly, I oversaw the support operations of the hospital. What's interesting about me working at the hospital is that I wasn't particularly looking for a job at the time. In fact, I would have never considered a position in the health-care field. I was initially recruited for the position by several guys who had previously worked for me and whom I had mentored earlier on in their lives.

They worked at Scripps, and when this position opened, they mentioned me as a person of interest. With my background in organizational development, I was highly qualified to take on this incredible responsibility, and I accepted the position. It can sometimes be a very challenging job, but working at a hospital is very rewarding. I continue to find ways to adapt to the challenges that come with dealing with ADHD in the workplace. For example, I am often in meetings for hours, and paying attention becomes very difficult. In the past, I would reflect on the limitations placed on me by having ADHD, yet I could also see many talents that I had that were a result of having such high energy from hyperactivity. For example, my high, endless energy has always made me a magnet for others. My ability to have a high sense of perception always helped me as a police officer where intuition was critical. In the workplace, it helped me to develop strong relationships and to take on complex projects that required my ability to work simultaneous projects without skipping a beat.

Back to my encounter with Anthony, our conversation continued.

"Would you like anything else? Adding a beverage to your order only adds seventy-five cents to your total," he informed me.

"Yes! I would also like a bottle of water," I responded.

It was going to be another warm day in La Jolla, California. I didn't want to leave Einstein Bros without something to quench my thirst. I had gone in with the intention of buying a beverage and would have been slightly disappointed in myself if I'd left without one. It was a good thing he mentioned it.

"For here or to go?"

I realized I'd forgotten to mention that as well. I took a closer look at the young man in front of me. He was so professional and attentive to my needs as a guest.

"To go," I replied.

"Would you like anything else?" he asked.

"No, that will be all."

"Okay. Today it's going to be $6.49, please."

I handed Anthony my credit card. He ran the card, and we continued making small talk as I waited for the credit card approval; all the while, I noted how busy it was in the store and how Anthony kept track of everything going on. He handed me my credit card receipt, which I signed and gave back to him. I watched him place all my items in a bag—the bagel, some butter, and extra napkins—and then he handed me the bag and my bottled water.

The breakfast rush had begun to form behind me. Although I should have just taken my bag and left, I know I didn't want to miss an opportunity to say something to this young man.

I was moved by his ability to connect with me right away. Although he seemed to lack self-confidence and hid behind his tough-guy look, I could sense on the inside that he was searching for a greater meaning for his life.

"I just want to thank you, I said. "You are very strong in customer service. It's almost as if you've read my mind. You made sure I had everything I needed before I left."

"Thanks," he responded. "I take my job seriously."

It was obvious that he did. However, it wasn't every day that I came across a young man who struck me as having so much potential. I wished I'd had a little bit more time to talk to him. I wondered what his future goals were. Did he always see himself working at Einstein Bros? Was he in school?

I knew that at the hospital, we were always looking to hire people like him. Plus, I thought it would be a great opportunity for him.

"That is great to see. Our hospital could use a person who takes his job seriously and puts customers first." I pulled my business card out of my jacket pocket and handed it to him. "Here is my card. If you are interested in a job, give me a call."

"Okay, thanks." It was all he was able to get out.

I quickly took one more look at his face before I left. It seemed as though he was in shock. I'm sure when he arrived at work that day, he never thought a random customer would offer him a position for another employer!

I have to admit this was not the first time I had reached out to someone whom I have had a short but powerful connection with. Even still, the experience is always profound. I knew I saw something in Anthony. I felt something with Anthony that I needed to explore further. I could only hope that he decided to call me. I couldn't wait to discuss the exciting things he was going to do with his future.

As I pushed through the front doors of Einstein Bros, I put my sunglasses back on. I delighted in the sunshine on my face and the knowledge that I may play a role in his life.

— — —

It was the end of another workday, and I was ready to relax. I could almost visualize myself being in the gym. Any activity such as racquetball was the perfect way for me to wind down and keep in shape.

Living a healthy lifestyle has always been very important to me. As I have seen others in their forties, I've taken note that my health is very good and realize it's to my advantage to keep fit. Even when I dine out, which tends to be often, foods such as salmon and roasted vegetables are consistent staples in my diet.

On this particular day, I decided to go straight home from the hospital and relax. All I needed to do was battle the five-o'clock traffic jam on the I-805, and I would be home free.

My phone rang, but it was a number I didn't recognize. I decide to pick it up. I met new people all the time, through work and my personal life, so getting a call from a number I didn't recognize was nothing out of the ordinary.

"Hello, this is Kevin," I answered.

"Hello, Kevin. This is Anthony. Not sure if you remember me."

I had not forgotten Anthony even though a few weeks had passed since our first encounter at Einstein Bros. That voice was very familiar to me, although he sounded a bit more nervous and uncertain.

"Of course I remember. From Einstein Bros Bagels, right?" I reassure him.

"Yeah, I met you a few weeks ago. I don't know if I took too long to call," he continued.

"No, Anthony. It's never too late. Thanks for deciding to give me a call. How can I help you?"

When the two of us had met, Anthony had asked how he could help me when I wanted a bagel. Now, I was in a position where I could help him. It felt gratifying for me.

"I just wanted to call and tell you that I'm interested in a job," he responded.

I had hoped that was why he was calling me. When I first left Einstein Bros, I had anticipated him calling me, but after a few days, I figured he wasn't interested. I knew it was a long shot to get someone who was good at his job to leave for another. But perhaps after thinking about it for a while, he decided he was open to other options.

I was excited about our possibilities.

"That is great," I said. "I just need you to write down my e-mail address. Then you can send me your résumé so I can look it over."

There was nothing but silence over the phone.

"I don't have one," he finally said.

It wasn't that unusual for a young man such as Anthony to not have a résumé. I was sure he at least had all of his information, because he would have been required to fill out an application for his current job. I realized I would just have to make sure he didn't become too discouraged by this.

"That's fine, Anthony," I said. "Is there a time we can meet up to talk, and I can help you create one?"

"Sure," he responded. "Where did you want to meet?"

"What area do you live in?"

"I live in City Heights."

I knew exactly where City Heights was. It was an area on the east side of San Diego. It was known for self-employed immigrant businesses and an ethnically diverse population. I knew all too well of the high rate of gang crimes in the neighborhood. My nonprofit organization, PowerMentor, provides services in this area. In fact, I decided to live near City Heights, so I could be close to the area that we serve.

The PowerMentor program targets the Latino population of southeastern San Diego, which is one of the most diverse communities in a city primarily occupied by Latinos. The area of Barrio Logan, where the PowerMentor organization was launched, is located in an area that was first settled by Mexicans in the 1890s. Shortly thereafter, refugees escaping the violence of the Mexican Revolution and poverty in their native countries sought safety in Barrio Logan. Barrio Logan remains a predominantly Latino community. Southeast San Diego is known for high crime rates, intense gang activity, and a high student dropout rate. PowerMentor has served this geographic area since 1996. While I work at the hospital during the week, my weekend hours are spent with PowerMentor.

I knew Anthony had already faced some hardships being from a rough neighborhood. I was hoping I could help him achieve the greatness he had inside him.

"Me too. How about meeting at the Starbucks on University and Fairmont? Does that work for you?" I asked.

"Yeah, that's near my house. It would be really convenient for me to walk there," he replied.

"Okay, how about tomorrow at six o'clock in the evening?"

"That works," he agreed. "See you then."

As I hung up the phone, I was excited that Anthony had decided to meet with me. I could already see a bright future for him and visualize that my meeting with Anthony would be the beginning of an amazing journey for him.

I could sense that Anthony probably came from a tough life, and I wondered what his goals in life might be. I was excited to meet him once again and see what dreams he had for his life.

— — —

I showed up a half hour early for my meeting with Anthony. I'm usually early for everything, just so I can prepare myself and have time to settle in. I always take time beforehand to try and visualize the mentee as he could be instead of seeing him as who he is now. I always reflect on the fact that when I was young, people would often tell my mother that I was going to be working in fast-food restaurants all my life, and that was if she were lucky. Others saw me for my weakness, and because of this experience, I committed myself to seeing others as what they could one day become. Instead of focusing on what people cannot do, I like to focus on what they can do, and I treat them accordingly.

I was aware that Anthony may have been bringing some hardships with him, but I was focused on what greatness he could achieve. I knew I saw something in him before, and I couldn't wait to get started.

As I spent my last few seconds alone, I said a quick prayer. I asked God to give me the right encouraging words to say to motivate and inspire Anthony to change his life. All my strength comes from God. I needed Him through this process too. Even though I am the mentor, I know I cannot do this without Him.

I took out my iPad and my computer and started setting everything up. I always carry my iPad with me, but today the computer was also necessary. I was hopeful that by the end of our time together, I would have a great résumé created for Anthony.

More importantly, I wanted to make sure I was ready to go when Anthony arrived. He didn't know much about me, so my strategy was for him to see a relaxed smile on my face right away.

As I walked to the Starbucks to meet with Anthony, I couldn't help but think back on why I started PowerMentor in the first place. I didn't know it at the time, but it really was about the ripple effect. I wanted to create a program that would make a chain of encouragement and motivation for young Latino men that would move them out of being a likely number on death or incarceration lists.

When Anthony walked in the door, he nervously looked around the Starbucks. He was right on time. He seemed to have changed his appearance to an extent from the day I had met him at Einstein Bros. He wore jeans, a fitted baseball cap, and an oversized T-shirt. He now had a very visible tattoo on his neck, which read: "Trust No Bitch."

I was incredibly taken aback by this. It immediately gave me insight into what kind of life he had been living. At the same time, it indicated to me that I may have had a very challenging task ahead of me. Nevertheless, I got up from my small table and greeted Anthony with a firm handshake, which he returned.

"Can I get you anything? Coffee? Water?" I asked as we took our seats. I wanted him to feel as comfortable as possible. I also wanted to let him know that I planned on staying awhile and really work collaboratively to figure out the plan for him.

"No," he said timidly. "I think I'm okay."

"Well, it's nice to see you, Anthony. Thank you for meeting with me. I'm interested to know, other than Einstein Bros, can you tell me what kind of experience you have? Are you in college?"

"I have only worked in restaurants, and I'm not in school," he responded.

A lot of young people start off in the restaurant industry. It's a business that has a fast turnover rate and offers on-the-job training. Even if Anthony didn't feel like this was an accomplishment, I knew it was. Through his restaurant experience, he had already mastered the skill of customer service. I knew there were other skills we could uncover as well.

Anthony seemed like such a smart individual. I hoped college would be a good fit for him. Unfortunately, Anthony was street smart, not book smart, so this gap would not be easily overcome. But I couldn't help but wonder: what if he did make that leap, and what if his life was forever changed?

"What about school? Do you have any plans?" I asked.

Anthony was surprisingly open with me. He was not hesitant to talk and share his life with a stranger. After talking for a while, it almost seemed like we had known each other for a long time.

"Probably not. I don't think it's for me—too expensive," he finally said.

I didn't think college would be out of Anthony's grasp. If Anthony didn't see it as a possibility, then maybe it was better that I reminded him about the original idea I had for him—working at the hospital.

"Have you thought about what kind of position you would like to have at the hospital? I know at Einstein Bros you work with the public a lot, and your experience in customer service could really qualify you for many positions. If that's something you still want to focus on, I think it would be a good fit for you. We have many opportunities available that we could look at."

"I'm not sure," he said, "Anything, I guess."

I knew that Anthony was better than what he was leading me to believe. I could sense he was holding back because he lacked a positive self-image. He had a calling in life. I could feel it. I just needed him to tell me what it was.

I didn't want him to think that I didn't see anything in him, because I did. I should have been asking him about what his future goals were. Maybe they didn't have anything to do with Einstein Bros, college, or the hospital. I wanted him to really open up to me.

"Anthony, let me ask you something. What is your goal for the future?"

"I always wanted to be a firefighter," he answered.

It all made sense to me. Firefighters are brave, courageous, and fearless. They put their lives on the line to save others. This was the greatness that Anthony was made to achieve. It was also something I could relate to.

"I am a former police officer myself," I told him. "Oftentimes, we would work with the fire department."

I was familiar with how Anthony could work his way to becoming a firefighter. I could help him the whole way through. Maybe I could even introduce him to a couple of friends of mine who are active firefighters.

"Really?"

I could tell Anthony was impressed.

"Yes," I assured him. "It is a very hard but rewarding job. It's quite a process to complete, but it's easy to get started. What is stopping you from achieving that dream?"

Anthony's excitement of becoming a firefighter quickly turned to disappointment. "I was convicted of a felony for robbery and was locked up in county jail for nine months, so I'm not sure if that will ever happen now."

I could see the embarrassment on his face as my heart sank.

A felony was going to hold him back from a lot of great jobs, especially being a firefighter. It made me sad to hear him say he had a felony, because I knew the implications and the barrier this would create for him. However, I was holding onto hope because I still had a feeling inside that there was a plan for him in all of this.

"Well, Anthony, that's not good, because to become a firefighter, you have to pass a background check. The felony will always prevent you from getting that job. And unfortunately, I would not be able to accept you for a job at the hospital for the same reason."

"That is what I figured. That's why it took me a couple weeks to call you. I knew I probably wouldn't be able to get a job. This felony keeps me from getting a lot of good jobs, even though it was a stupid thing that happened in the first place. I decided to call you anyway, because it's been awhile since someone saw something in me. I was hoping you could help me in some way, because sometimes I do get scared about my future."

I agreed that Anthony was being held back because of the felony. He could achieve so many great things in this life, and I was glad he saw something in me too and decided to reach out. I had helped so many people in similar situations. I just needed to find out exactly what he was struggling with and what I could do.

"Anthony, first let me tell you that I do not think it is an accident that we are meeting today. I believe you are in the world for a specific purpose."

"I also feel like there is a reason why our paths crossed." He agreed. "I feel like it was destined to happen."

"Yes! Because I believe there is a greater plan and purpose for your life. Your future is in your hands. It is all about the decisions you make. I have known others guys who had felony convictions and went on to do amazing things in their lives. So I am encouraging you to not get discouraged. I still feel like I may be able to help."

"If you could help in any way, it would be good. Right now, it's kind of hard when I am stuck working at fast-food restaurants. I know my situation is probably a lot to handle."

I took a second to reflect on my own past. I had been in this situation before with other guys. Anthony shouldn't feel like he was alone.

"Anthony, I have worked with convicted felons in the past. I have helped men with similar situations as you turn their lives around."

To really help Anthony, I needed to know everything. I needed to know who he was, where he came from, and what happened to get him that felony.

"What was the crime that you were convicted of?" I asked.

"I was convicted of attempted robbery."

Wow. Attempted robbery. That was pretty serious. I had to try to keep a straight face. I didn't want Anthony to think that I was judging him before we started. I also didn't want him to think it was more than I could handle. Even with the felony, it was a less serious circumstance than I was used to dealing with. I knew I could handle it.

"Okay, tell me exactly what happened. Walk me through it."

Anthony's demeanor changed as he reflected back to that night. I could still see the pain in his face. It was clear to me that this event was still traumatizing him now that he knew the consequences of having a felony.

"City Heights can be pretty rough. Sometimes, you really feel like you have to constantly look behind your back. The best way to survive in my neighborhood is to stand by your friends and stick up for one another. I don't always agree with the fighting and the violence, but you don't turn away from what you know. That can get you into even more trouble."

"So when my friend said he was having a disagreement with a guy from another crew, I knew I needed to help him out. We all gathered face-to-face to work things out. We were just supposed to talk. It turned into a fight. The cops were called, and all of us got arrested.

"In jail, I was told I was being charged with strong-arm robbery, which is a felony. Turns out that during the fight, my friend grabbed the guy's chain from around his neck and broke it off. It was an accident. A lot of things happen spur of the moment. He didn't mean to do it. The 'victim' said we were trying to take his property.

"Since I was eighteen at the time of the fight, they were able to charge me as an adult. I was taken to jail, I lost my job, and my life was over."

Anthony told me his story. It turned out that he'd been jammed up on felony charges during a fight on the street. Instead of a felony, the charges should have been misdemeanor battery at most. I was pretty annoyed. Sometimes the legal system eats people up and spits them out with no compunction whatsoever.

"So you actually weren't robbing him for the chain. It was just a fight that ended with damaged property?" I asked.

"Exactly. Why would we risk so much for a stupid chain necklace?"

"Did you hire an attorney?

"I was given a public defender," he said.

"What did your public defender say?"

"He said the district attorney was planning on going after me. There was a good chance I would be found guilty. If I were convicted, they could have sentenced me to up to ten years in prison. It would be better if I just pleaded guilty."

I couldn't believe what Anthony was telling me. He would live the rest of his life with a record that did not fit the crime. He was raised in a community where no one gave him a chance, and the system treated him like a product of his environment.

"Did you tell your public defender exactly what you told me?" I questioned.

"Yes, but he said no one would believe me. If I pleaded guilty, I could go home. I didn't want to stay in jail anymore, so I did it. I didn't even know what it meant to plead guilty to a felony. No one explained it to me before I handed in my plea. I had no idea how it was going to change my life."

It was sad. Not even his public defender believed in him. But I did. I had the feeling that Anthony and I had met for a reason, and this was it. I was going to help him achieve his dream. After hearing Anthony's story, I had a better feeling about being able to get this felony reduced to a misdemeanor. Hopefully one day, I would be able to remove that barrier from his life.

"I hear you, Anthony," I told him. "I know it must have been tough. But today is the first day of the rest of your life! What decision you make from today forward will determine your future. I believe you can do great things."

"Kevin, I grew up on the streets of City Heights. I hang out with guys that are in gangs, and I like that life, you know? It's what I know. It's what I'll always be. Jail or death, whichever comes first. Everything is set up against me, so I don't stand a chance."

Anthony must have been convinced that the only way to move on with his life was to settle.

"Anthony, you say that, but I can sense you are not happy with your life right now. I think you are not content, and you know there is something better out there for you. Deep down, you know you can do more in this life."

There was a silence between us as he struggled to find something to object to. This had to be the first time that Anthony had been challenged to do great things. He could try to fight my method, but he was slowly learning I was right.

"I don't know. I try not to think about it. I just work as hard as I can and chill with my friends. I don't really think about my future."

I could feel the encouragement pour out of me. He was full of potential and just needed to believe in himself. I knew he wanted to change. I could see it in him.

"Why don't you see a future for yourself?" I asked. "Your future is in your hands based on the decisions you make. You can play the victim all you want, but your decisions are what have caused the dilemmas in your life. Anthony, there are consequences for every action you chose, both positive and negative.

"I see something in you that tells me you can break away from the life you had and the life you see for yourself. I want to get to know you better and help you see things a little bit differently. Will you open your mind up and let me help you see your life in another way?"

I saw all of Anthony's walls begin breaking down. As he shared, I could sense he had been holding so much inside for many years, and he found someone he could trust to not judge him.

"Kevin, I do want to change," he admitted. "Maybe my life will change now."

A feeling of excitement rushed over me. All of our discussion had paid off. Anthony was on board for changing his life and having a bright future.

I felt humbled by the fact that he was going to let me embrace this change with him. I now had the responsibility of trying to mentor someone who needed to transform everything about himself—his mind, his decisions, everything.

Now the tough part began.

"Anthony, some of the things I'm going to tell you, you may not like. I'm going to ask you to hear me out, though.

"First, you are your own worst enemy. I can't tell you how many people I know who are just like you, and even more who are worse off. Yet, they made it and have done amazing things in their lives.

They've gone to school, landed incredible jobs, and now have families of their own."

"They couldn't have been like me," he noted.

"Yes, Anthony. Guys your age with your circumstances, your background, and your mentality. They were very similar to you. You would be stunned if I told you how strikingly similar some of the guys are to you who have changed their lives forever.

"There is a plan for your life, Anthony. All you have to do is find your purpose and put your eyes on your goals, and you will do it! I will walk alongside you the entire way to encourage you and give you guidance."

"I've never had anyone tell me these kinds of things. Are you sure you can help?"

"Today is your day. You get to choose your future and make your dreams come true." I picked up a small journal that I'd brought with me. I showed it to Anthony as I started flipping through it. "Do you see this, Anthony? It's a notebook filled with real experiences I have had with guys just like you. I'm writing a book based on overcoming adversity and fulfilling dreams. By the end of writing this book, I want your felony charge to be cleared completely. That's how much I believe in you. That's how much I'm willing to fight for you."

Anthony was ecstatic. There was no turning back now for us.

"I'm in. What do I have to do?" he asked.

"Just answer a question. Are you ready for this change?"

Chapter Two

Others Have Done It, and So Can You

A few weeks later, I met with Anthony yet again. We had been meeting more and more frequently at the Starbucks by my house because it was a convenient location for both of us.

As the time of our meeting approached, I looked outside to see if he was coming. Sure enough, Anthony and a group of young guys were walking toward Starbucks. Once outside the door, he gave each a unique handshake as they disappeared.

As Anthony was about to walk in, I stood up to greet him. "Hi, Anthony. Thanks for coming."

"Yeah, thanks. I was excited about meeting with you today," he responded.

"As am I."

As we took our seats, I knew I had to confront Anthony with some tough questions. "Anthony, if you don't mind me asking, who were those guys you were walking with?"

"Oh, those guys are my closest friends."

"Was your friend there? The one from the night of the fight when you got arrested?"

"Yeah."

I was curious as to why Anthony would still want to hang around with a friend who had already gotten him in so much trouble. If it weren't for him, Anthony could have become a firefighter with no problems.

"And what are they up to these days? Any of them in school or have jobs?"

Anthony was hesitant to tell me the answer. I was sure he knew what I was up to.

"Um, about the same as me," he answered. "Working minimum-wage jobs; some sell drugs on the side. They are just doing what they can to survive. We are all at a disadvantage in life."

Instead of breaking free from his friends, Anthony found their felony as a way to bond. He needed to move on and correct his life, not stick up for his friends who were still into trouble. He couldn't compare his hardships to other hardships. He needed to separate himself from the bad lifestyle.

"No, Anthony, you are not. You are better than those friends and that mentality. You want to change, right? You want to be more than just living paycheck to paycheck? More than a man with a record?"

"Yeah, of course."

"Then the first step in your new life is going to be breaking away from those 'friends.'"

I saw something new in Anthony that I had never seen before—refusal.

"No way. I'm not doing it," he said. "Those are my boys, my brothers. We've been through everything together, good and bad. We stand by each other no matter what. I can't just walk away from them. We are bonded together for life by what we have been through. No one will ever understand me the way they do. I could never be close with anyone else."

Anthony had the wrong mentality when it came to his friends. They weren't bonded together; they were holding each other down.

"Anthony, real friends will help each other succeed. Real friends will encourage you to brighten your future. If you better your life, then your friends should be there for you. You need to stop the cycle you're in. Because of your friends, you already have one felony on your record. Imagine what else could happen if their habits continue."

"I can still be on a path for myself and keep my friends."

"I understand where you are coming from, Anthony. You have a yearning to be a part of a group. It's what our identity is. You have to realize that your friends are going to have a very strong influence on the decisions you make in your life. They might be strong enough to hold you back. Let me ask you something. Did you tell your friends why you coming here today?" I asked. This would be a true test for him.

"No," he quietly said.

I already knew the answer. I also knew why he hadn't said anything to them. Interestingly, most people stereotypically believe that gang-involved young people are evil, dishonest, and not worthy. In reality, my experience has been that the Anthonys of the world will respond to how they are treated. If I showed him trust and respect, I would gain that in return. One of my favorite quotes and something I live by comes from Johann Wolfgang Von Goethe: "Treat people as if they were what they ought to be, and you help them to become what they are capable of being."

"Why not?" I asked.

Anthony didn't say anything. I knew what he was thinking. His friends wouldn't support him. They would put him down.

"Anthony, it is so critical that you align yourself with people who believe in what you can do instead of those shallow people who are focused on telling you what you can't do. When you do the very thing that you said you couldn't do, they will find every fault in what you did do. They will critique your every intent and action."

"My friends aren't like that," he replied.

"Believe me. There will always be opposition from people around you, especially from people who are living in the average, the content, the stagnant, and the mediocre. These are the people that no matter what you do, there is no pleasing them. This is because the more you do, the more they are confronted with the fact that you are a can-do person, while they are steeped in the can't-do rut."

"You must not really know me or my friends. We will stick by each other no matter what," Anthony contended. "My crew ain't like that! You got it all wrong." Anthony gripped the table with both hands and leaned forward. His eyes glinted with anger and pent-up emotion.

If I hadn't worked with lots of gang-involved individuals like him before, I might have actually been scared, even as an ex-cop. I told him to relax, that I was only making a point and he'd do well to listen.

"You think you know it all. You don't. You don't know jack shit," Anthony said as he got up to leave. "I'm outta here. Thanks for nothin'."

"If your friendship has the proper foundation, it will withstand anything. Nothing can come between those bonds. However, the friendships you created in your life have been forged through this need to fill the void in your life. Something in your life has turned you to the gang life. That's not the proper foundation that will last in your friendships."

"Maybe not with your friends, but it works for me."

I knew Anthony's type too well. I had seen it before. He thought he was different from the other guys I'd met, but he wasn't. I decided to use the experience of my past to let him know how friends can influence you to make the wrong decision. Staying loyal to the wrong friends can take you to the wrong places.

He looked me right in the eye and said, "What makes you think PowerMentor could help me?"

I told Anthony all about PowerMentor, what it did, and why I founded it. He questioned how PowerMentor could make a difference in his life; after all, there were so many programs out there.

"Well, Anthony, first of all, I never classify PowerMentor as a program, but instead, it is a concept, a model of leading others through what I call vertical learning. Vertical learning is the transformation of how leaders think, feel, and make sense of the world. It includes the development of both mental complexity and emotional intelligence, which is our ability to understand how others perceive us. We can accelerate our learning by understanding that 'how we know' is more important than 'what we know,' especially when leading through complex change. Effective leaders of the future must be highly strategic thinkers able to focus on complex problems and opportunities, superb and inspiring communicators with excellent people skills, risk-oriented, and deeply collaborative. Because we see youth as future leaders, our strategy is to develop future leaders one person at a time. This is so that individuals are empowered to break through the glass ceiling, cultivate high-impact innovation, build high-trust relationships, act with deep courage, and have the ability to transform themselves, others, and the organizations they will one day lead.

"Anthony, let me share with you what others have noted in their experiences with PowerMentor. It may resonate with you and help you understand this journey. For example, twenty-year-old Adan explained his PowerMentor experience as something so new that he had never experienced anything like it before. I want to share something that Adan wrote to give you his insight."

I then read the following firsthand account to Anthony:

> My experience with PowerMentor was a whole new thing for me. It's different, not like having a counselor,

but instead it was all about the personal experience with the mentors and seeing how they supported one another.

The level of encouragement was so unreal, like nothing I have ever felt before. They were so in tune with what I had been through in my life and what I needed to accomplish my future goals. The constant encouraging me to press forward with school and putting the right people around me and staying away from the wrong people. These things sound basic but empowered me so much. As a mentee, it was obvious to me that all of these mentors believed in me and saw something great in me. Instead of just telling me how to do things, they showed me! They talked about things that seem so basic; yet, I had never heard much of it before. I was not used to people getting to know me for who I am. The mentors went deeper than that, and that was new because no one had ever gone that deep in understanding me. One of the main things that they did was encourage, encourage, encourage … and they never, ever gave up on you. Seeing how interested PowerMentor was toward me, that made me become more interested in school and my goals to get ahead.

The amazing part of my experience was that they also could see when I would progress. When I did, they would provide something that I needed for the next part of my journey. For example, for college, I really needed a laptop computer so I could do work from home. PowerMentor provided a computer for me, and not only did it make things so much easier for me, but it was the fact that they again showed me through action that they were behind me and believed in me so much. To make that investment in me had a great impact on me. It just showed me that they really wanted me to succeed. It wasn't something to uplift themselves; it was more to get me to do good, to succeed, to show me that I could do much more than what I thought.

Growing up as a Latino, you grow up with the knowledge that as long as you have what you need, you're okay. If you get comfortable with what you have, often you never try to go above that. PowerMentor showed me otherwise; they showed me that I could do much more than just the status quo.

Some of the barriers that we also face as Latinos include the stereotypes that that we don't get far in life and that we basically are good for jobs that require physical labor without intelligence. That discourages us from reaching upward for a better life. Unfortunately, many Latino families are the culprit in furthering this, because the tradition and norm in Latino families is that at a certain age we should be working in restaurants or construction, finding a spouse, and having kids, all as young as possible. It's something that's implied. You get a labor job once you turn eighteen and are expected to help your parents pay the bills. If you have other siblings, sometimes you're expected to provide things for them, such as clothing or anything they need, basic things.

These things can get very stressful, because sometimes parents, without understanding the need to attend college, can put a guilt trip on you and make you feel bad for not doing things they want you to do such as working full-time without going to college. You drop everything that you're doing, such as school, to meet a parent's expectation. Sometimes instead of going to apply at a school, you go and apply for a job. Instead of taking the time to learn a skill that helps you secure a career in the future, you're learning how to cook food for a restaurant. It's either you go to school, or you find a job to start providing. You basically become a provider as soon as you graduate from high school and are old enough to work.

It was very helpful to have mentors understand this cultural challenge because they too experienced the same thing as me. Having the ability to talk to someone to release what I had inside was very helpful. The ability to get sound advice was always a huge relief for many of us.

Latinos really need motivation and inspiration, because we lack that within our culture. It is not talked about within our families like it could be. Sometimes as Latinos we lack motivation to graduate high school. At a high-school level, you are not pressured to get a job or anything; basically, your only job is to be good, respect your parents, and do well in school.

There are those who would just have a hard time with school. With anything, we need someone to do homework with, someone who would say, "Hey, you want to go do some homework?"

More than anything, in school you can do work because you have teachers telling you, "Hey, finish your work. Finish your work." But once you get home, who's telling you? Your parents, they tell you to do your homework, but many of us just say yes and really do not do it. Why? Because they don't know what our homework is; we don't understand. We can show them a page of our notes, and they would say, "Oh, that's your homework. Very good." We would get by, and then we just go do whatever we want.

However, when we have someone who understands what our homework is and who can keep us accountable as a high-school student, that's a big help. We need accountability, and the way PowerMentor provided that was really good. Every weekend you could count on a group doing their college homework at a local Starbucks, and everyone was encouraged to join in. The mentors would give us a call. "Hey, did you do your homework?" Taking the time, even if it was only an hour out of their day or just open up a study group program, a site where they might provide help or we could just go and be, "Hey, it's homework time," that was so helpful.

One of the other things that was a plus with PowerMentor was how they helped us keep going to college or go to college or stay in college by helping us with the basic stuff, like a bus pass. Many of us don't have a means of transportation. A ride was definitely helpful. I remember when for the longest time Kevin would pick me up on his way to work and drop me off at college. Not only was it transportation, but he had a way of encouraging me every morning! He would pick me up, and we would go by Starbucks for a drink and breakfast sandwich and talk about anything that was going on. He would ask me how I was doing and encourage me by instilling in me that there was a purpose for my life, and he would be excited to hear how I was progressing through my journey. Every day, he did not skip a beat. That was not only a commitment on his part, but it was very meaningful to me. If Kevin had not picked me up as he did, I would have had to wake up an hour and a half earlier just to get to school at the same time via the bus. I now had enough time to finish unfinished homework or time to study before a big test. PowerMentor would help me purchase expensive textbooks that were required for my classes. Textbooks are expensive, and as a Latino who was undocumented at the time, I did not receive any financial aid or have the ability to work to pay for the material. Sometimes we can't afford the books, because sometimes the book is more expensive than the class itself.

For me, to have a mentor take an interest in me was good. I was up for it. The relationship wasn't just that they were my mentors, and I was the mentee. It was more: you're my friend, and I'm your friend. It wasn't a formal-type thing; it was personal, and it was real. I know your name; I know some of your likes, interests, hobbies; and I know why you have those interests and why you have those hobbies. It was so authentic. It was no longer just a mentor-mentee type of relationship; it was more of a leading-type relationship.

For me, I just made a friend. I no longer viewed the mentors as somebody who was just teaching me, but I saw a friend coming alongside of me who was helping me, and I saw that they were also learning from me. That made it so powerful, because I was never made to feel like I was some poor guy who needed a handout. It was a partnership, and they were investing in me and asking me in turn to invest in others. The pass-it-on theme.

PowerMentor genuinely cared about me. They did not try and tell me what to do. They learned what I was passionate about and then helped me navigate toward that. That was always crystal clear. Many times we would strategize about my life informally. He would say, "Hey, you want to get some dinner, some lunch, some coffee?"

The mentors never realized how great their timing was. I would be at a low point, and all of a sudden I would get this call, as if they knew I was down. It was the craziest thing. During the dinner, lunch, or coffee, I was able to talk to my mentors and tell them what was going on with me, what was going on in my life. If I had certain problems, I shared them. I was able to get things off my chest, get advice—many different things aside from homework. We would also, at times, just do homework, work on projects, or whatever. They all helped each other in what they were working on; it was a part of the PowerMentor culture. That was something; I've never been part of any experience like this, and the events that the mentors were involved in were really big. It gave me purpose knowing that I was a part of it. They would do things like movie nights in the park, and hundreds of people would show up. It was really something that impacted me every time I was with them.

For example, there's a difference between just showing up to an event and being part of the team that has planned the event to begin with. Being part of an event was to get to know the people who set up the event, and you get to know their stories, why they were doing this, their reasons. Sometimes those reasons really impacted me. Wow! It was so inspirational, so motivating, causing me to want to step out and lead an event myself. It made me want to do something big.

Being part of some of the events that had some of the mentors as presenters was almost like interviewing someone—being there and listening to them personally, not just through a recording. It was like they were talking directly to me. Sometimes the things they said applied to me so much; it was so deep.

I remember one such event that was a memorial service for a young kid who was killed. I met the family of the victim and the people who had set up the event and was able to know them on a personal level. Somehow PowerMentor would turn a sad moment like someone being killed into a transformational call to action for those attending to consider their own lives and make positive changes to impact their world. People would cry and would commit themselves to changing their lives and being a positive influence. The way they would engage large numbers of people was very interesting to me. I would reflect, asking myself, "How did they do this so well and make it look so easy?"

An opportunity that stood out to me most was when Kevin asked me to help shoot video for an event he planned for an individual from the Karen community. These people were violently persecuted in Burma and escaped with their lives coming to the United States as refugees. Several of them wanted to become missionary nurses and learn how to fly so they could provide humanitarian relief back in their country as medical missionaries in the future. Kevin would take them flying for the first time. It was amazing, because I was able to see how this came to fruition and then come to completion. One of the Karen guys had shared with Kevin his dream, and a few days later, I see Kevin arranging things. He called a friend of his named Bruce who was a commercial pilot and flight instructor. Bruce had a story of his own too. He was originally from Burundi, a war-torn region in Africa. Kevin seemed to always be thinking ahead. Everything was always a strategy. I remember him on the phone planning and telling Bruce how he would have the opportunity to impact others who had also experienced violence in their war-torn region. I could sense Bruce was excited, and it was locked in. We were scheduled for a Saturday morning flight.

I later learned that Kevin asked me to shoot video for him because he knew I had never flown before, and he wanted me to experience flying. So think about that: Kevin strategically planned to have me impacted by experiencing flying for the first time, while Bruce would be impacted by helping young men who had experienced what he had when he was younger, and finally the Karen guys would recognize the beginning of their dream to one day become pilots flying medical missions in their home country. Amazing!

The day of the flight, I saw everything that Kevin had planned come to fruition like clockwork. The ability PowerMentor has with connecting with so many people—it's just unreal. I never thought for a moment that I would one day be flying in a plane, looking outside from high in the sky. Hearing the Karen guys share their experiences of violence in their country and why they wanted to become missionary nurse pilots was something else. Wow! Look, I'm flying. We were all meticulously engaged in such a special way, orchestrated by Kevin who seemed to just take it in his stride, as if it were just another normal day for him.

The flight was amazing, and I will never forget that experience—not only the flight, but it was the first time I was given a glimpse into how Kevin thinks and plans things to have very specific impact on others. Being part of the event made me feel more alive and purposeful. I was part of something greater than myself. It was not just the plane; it was the people who were impacted, all while Kevin seemed to take it as an everyday occurrence. Yet, to all of us, it was something we'd never felt before.

I have also come to learn how to have a different perspective and keep things in the proper context. I used to stress over things and now have learned that much of what I stressed about I have no control over. Instead, I now focus on what I can control and the stress seems to be at a minimum.

I'm actually interested; for once in my life, I'm interested in school. I used to think it was just, *Yeah, school is good for me. It's going to benefit me in my life, so I'll just get through it and just do well so it can do me good.* I had no real core desire to do something with my life until PowerMentor impacted me. They didn't tell you what you should do; they asked the right questions to help you conclude that for yourself. When they saw potential in something they observed in me, they would say, "Hey, you'd be pretty good doing this." But they would never say, "You should do this. Just stick to this, and you'll be good." It was more, "Hey, you're pretty good at this. You're interested. You seem to be pretty good."

That got me thinking, *Hey, I am pretty good at this, and I like this.* Each time, there was never pressure that I had to do something.

At the same time, they help other people with the same story and see how they're doing. Sometimes they feed off each other. For example, many Latinos grow up without dads. Many times, we almost take the role of dad in our households, especially the oldest. If you're the oldest, it's much harder; it's tough. There's a reason why I'm the oldest. I'm not always completely sure, but for some reason, I'm there.

Meeting somebody else that has a similar background as me and, even at times, they may be the oldest as well. As I hear how they got through the difficult times in their lives, it helps me get through my stress.

One time, I asked myself why it is that I don't cry or miss my dad or anything anymore. What I realized is that I am more mature now, and in a sense, I had to mourn my loss. One of the biggest ways that they helped me want to graduate was by helping me realize many things, and by having us meet other people who have similar situations, that helps us. We encourage one another, and sooner or later, we're both graduating and at the top. Within PowerMentor, the success people have is really something. Some are lawyers and about to do much more, and all of that, all of their stories, are very encouraging. Some of them have the same background, and I want to be able to do something big someday too.

One of the things that I found very big with PowerMentor has to do with their involvement with me as an individual in that they sparked an interest, and then I became interested and wanting to help others as well. Just as they helped me, I want to help somebody else—someone who's also struggling the way I did, maybe even worse.

I just hope that how they helped me and how I want to help somebody else, I hope that the person whom I help wants to help somebody else as well. That it just becomes a chain of encouragement and motivation, so the whole statistic of Latino males having the highest high school dropout rate and lowest college entrance would change.

By doing this, more of us Latinos would be willing to go to school, and more of us would go to school and continue our education and make something of our lives. That's something that PowerMentor is doing. Something that they help with is that by encouraging one person and then that person passes it to another person, which that person could pass it to other two people, and it just becomes a chain.

I've seen many mentees; I've seen them want to help somebody else. They say, "I want to be a mentor. I got help, and I want to help somebody else as well just the way that they helped me." It's amazing. Not everybody is willing to do it, and it takes a handful of extraordinary people who want to help others to succeed. By helping others, it helps me stay accountable for my success too, because I know other are watching me or depending on me.

I paused for a moment to make sure that everything I was saying was sinking in with Anthony. Then I continued. "Over this process, can I share with you a few stories about some guys who were just like you?" I asked.

"Sure," he said.

"I know you better than you think I do. I think these stories will help you understand that I knew people just like you. They went on to accomplish great things."

"Yeah, tell me."

"Okay, now these stories will be hard for you to believe. In fact, at times, I still can't believe what I am getting ready to tell you, but when you meet these guys, you will see for yourself that everything I am about to tell you is true! First, there is the story of a man named Lalo Gunther. He reminds me a lot of you, because he too had a great loyalty to his friends. It was a loyalty that eventually got him into a lot of trouble."

I met then fourteen-year-old Lalo back in 1992 when I was a police officer for the El Cajon Police Department. He was from a gang-infested area of El Cajon, and I would come across him from time to time on my routine patrol. I was always asking him what he was up to and if he was staying out of trouble.

I knew he had come from a broken family and lived in a rough neighborhood. His parents had split up by the time he was two. He would only see his father every once in a while. The responsibility of both disciplinarian and nurturer fell on his mother. Although he knew his mother cared for him, Lalo lacked a fully functional, loving family structure.

He was so young and already showed so many signs of leading a life of crime and prison. This was due to the fact that his father was never around to show him how to grow and become an adult. Lalo felt he had to become a man on his own. All I could do was watch from a distance and hope he took my advice.

He had been kicked out of traditional high school and had tried living with different friends and family members. I always knew he was involved in the gang scene. For Lalo, he was trying to find his identity. He needed to belong somewhere. One day, Lalo found himself at odds with a Chaldean family in the neighborhood who had emigrated from Iraq. When he was showing up to resolve the fight, he saw a huge family show up in support of the Iraqis. When the gang members decided to stand by him, he was thankful. This was the perfect opportunity for him to bond with the guys he always saw hanging out around the neighborhood.

I tried to help him over the course of a few years. I patrolled the neighborhood where he lived when I was on duty as a police officer. I tried to get to know as many of the gang members as I could. I encouraged them to get involved in positive, constructive activities.

It's hard to believe that when I met Lalo at just fourteen years old, he had already joined a gang, been kicked out of high school, been placed on probation, and had been locked up by the California Youth

Authority after I had arrested him. When he was seventeen, his life forever changed.

"He hung around a lot of friends who were just like yours," I explained to Anthony.

"How?" he asked.

I continued. "When I questioned Lalo about his friends, he told me they were everything to him. He could not break away from them. I told him they would be his downfall. Whenever I got calls about discrepancies around the neighborhood, Lalo and his friends were never too far behind. I shared with him that if he did not chose right from wrong, then he would endure consequences that would be far reaching. He told me that he knew that he would always have his friends.

"He ignored my plea, and one week later, his friends asked him to take a dangerous ride with them. He agreed. That night, they were involved in a drive-by shooting. A young man, who was also a father, was almost killed. He was rushed to the hospital with gunshot wounds and had to undergo many surgeries to survive. After a tough struggle and long road of rehabilitation, the young man recovered.

"The worst part of the story? This was a random act of violence! Lalo and his friends did not even know who this man was. They shot and almost killed a complete stranger and someone who didn't deserve to die. And because of that, Lalo was arrested, charged as an adult for attempted murder, and sent to prison!"

I recounted the story for Anthony at the Starbucks located in one of the highest gang crime areas—so fitting. Anthony appeared surprised, especially about the fact that I'd had that kind of involvement with others like him.

"Wait. He had nothing to do with it? He didn't pull the trigger?" he asked in shock.

"No. He didn't know anyone would be hurt that night, but he was still charged because he was in the car."

"That is exactly what happened to me."

"I know," I said. "When he really needed his friends, they were nowhere to be found. In fact, they had the opportunity to help him, and they didn't. Just like your friends could have come forward about your situation and tried to prevent your felony from happening."

I then told Anthony more of Lalo's story. Following the drive-by shooting, Lalo and his friends remained strong. However, after being arrested, the police asked for everyone's side of the story. Lalo thought for sure that his friends would make sure he didn't see jail time, because he truly was not the one who pulled the trigger. He found that at the end of the day, it was every man for himself. Lalo was sentenced to seven years in prison, simply for sticking by his friends. Worse yet, the district attorney was trying to make an example out of Lalo and asked for life in prison with no chance of a plea bargain.

I wished he had listened to me, because I turned out to be the only person who stood by him during the process. I wrote to him all the time. I didn't sugarcoat the truth. He knew I was disappointed in him. I had lived with many disappointing decisions from Lalo. However, I let him know I wasn't going anywhere. I forgave him and told him that we would get through this together. Over the next several years, while he was incarcerated, I worked with Lalo to help him find the right path.

At first, he didn't want to accept the process. Even at that point, he felt like most of the blame should be placed on the police officers. They wanted to put him in prison. They didn't care about his side of the story.

I knew I couldn't help Lalo out of prison, and wouldn't want to, as he needed to be held responsible. I couldn't change the past. What I could do was change the future. Lalo was a very smart guy who liked experiencing adventure, watching movies, and working with people.

I asked him about what he'd thought his life would be like. He said he always pictured himself moving out of the neighborhood he lived in. He wanted to get married and have kids. He even thought he would have been the first kid in his family to go to college. It was clear that he had a good vision and that being a street kid was not a desire he had.

I believed in Lalo more than he believed in himself. I had to become a role model for him so he had something to strive for. We therefore built a connection that was based on belief in him and trust within each other. I involved him in work that we were doing in the community. He found a purpose in wanting to help the community and in helping others.

"I saw something in him just like I see something in you," I told Anthony. "I knew Lalo would achieve great things as long as he was willing to change."

"That could have been me. I could have a felony conviction *and* be serving time."

"That could still be you, Anthony. You have the same friends that could ask you to get into that car with them. And you would because of your distorted loyalty mind-set. You have the chance now to change your life before it gets to that point."

I went on to tell Anthony the rest of Lalo's story. "Lalo would finally choose the right path, but he still had to endure being incarcerated and having a felony conviction. The great thing about Lalo was that once he saw the light, he never turned back no matter how difficult that path became. He endured great trials because of his newfound life. Lalo found that prison took the same form as his life outside of prison. People form groups of friends and do dangerous things to prove their loyalty for one another.

"When fellow inmates would demand he take part in fights and jailhouse politics, he would refuse. He focused every day on making himself better. Because of this, maybe people saw him as weak and a traitor. Many inmates thought they could break him and turn him back into the person he was when he first went to jail. On one occasion, he even experienced the beating of his life.

"Lalo stayed strong and even tried sending the message of a bright, successful future to others around him. But the key is to believe in yourself and the process. You can't fake it. If you too want this process Anthony, then I can help you."

"Did it help Lalo?" he asked. "Did you help Lalo?"

"Lalo was released from prison after serving five years of his seven-year sentence. Because of his good behavior and letters to the appeals board that many of us wrote, he didn't have to serve his entire ten-year sentence. He served his prison time from June 1995 until his release in June 2000.

"When we heard of his release, I was overjoyed about his bright future. This was the moment we had been waiting for. He asked if I would be the one who picked him up from prison. I will never forget that day. After so long behind bars, he had nothing. He had no money in his pocket and only had the clothes on his back.

"This would be the tough part. Lalo had to be in charge of that change. He also wanted to get a college degree, and we weren't going to stop until he had the diploma in his hand. We had a plan for what we needed to do. First, Lalo had only completed high school, so we worked every day on getting him ready for college. Helping him adjust to the discipline of homework and working full-time to pay his expenses while attending college would be challenging.

"A friend from Lalo's church was able to get him a job working in a warehouse and didn't mind hiring Lalo to do some work. I knew after being convicted of a felony and serving time, it was going to be hard to find a job. I was thankful that his friend was able to get him this position.

"Lalo worked during the day and studied at night. The goal that we set while he was in prison to work hard and stay focused really paid off for us. Lalo was able to take night classes at a local community college and established a great GPA. I felt Lalo was ready to make that next step, so he submitted an application to San Diego Christian College and eagerly waited for the response. He was accepted.

"He was officially a college student. Lalo would be able to complete his dream of becoming the first member of his family to graduate from college. He would enter into college and receive a bachelor's degree in human development and continue his studies with a master's degree in divinity. At San Diego Christian College, he met amazing friends and even began dating a wonderful woman. He went on to further his education and established himself in the working world. Today Lalo is seeking his doctorate!

"Do you see, Anthony? Lalo went on to earn his bachelor's and master's and is continuing toward his doctorate. Now he is happily married with three children. His life was forever changed! He now has everything that he dreamt about having in prison. His old friends are still serving time and hustling on the streets. He doesn't miss that life or those people at all. He doesn't need to be friends with them, because they don't have the same new mind-set that Lalo has. Lalo is no longer in to the dangerous lifestyle. He surrounds himself with people who have the same goals and ambitions as him."

"You think he was able to do this because he left his friends behind?" Anthony asked.

"Yes, absolutely," I told him. "His friends saw his progress. They could have done the same thing he did. They chose not to, so they will always lead a life of crime and prison time unless they too decide to change their mind-sets."

I took out a piece of paper that I carry around with me for my first meetings. It serves as inspiration for those who don't believe in themselves because they are too busy wondering what other people will think.

"Anthony, I'd like you to read this out loud. It's an excerpt from Theodore Roosevelt's 'Man in the Arena'" speech that he delivered in Paris, France, on April 23, 1910."

Anthony took the paper from my hand and began to read.

"It is not the critic who counts: not the man who points out how the strong man stumbles or where the doer of deeds could have done better. The credit belongs to the man who is actually in the arena, whose face is marred by dust and sweat and blood, who strives valiantly, who errs and comes up short again and again, because there is no effort without error or shortcoming, but who knows the great enthusiasms, the great devotions, who spends himself for a worthy cause; who, at the best, knows, in the end, the triumph of high achievement, and who, at the worst, if he fails, at least he fails while daring greatly, so that his place shall never been those cold and timid souls who knew neither victory nor defeat …

"The man who really counts in the world is the doer, not the mere critic—the man who actually does the work, even if roughly and imperfectly, not the man who only talks or writes about how it ought to be done.

"Criticism is necessary and useful; it is often indispensable, but it can never take the place of action, or be even a poor substitute for it. The function of the mere critic is of very subordinate usefulness. It is the doer of deeds who actually counts in the battle for life, and not the man who looks on and says how the fight ought to be fought, without himself sharing the stress and the danger."

Anthony looked a little lost. I knew it was a lot of information to absorb in one sitting, so I explained what it meant to me.

"What this passage says to me is that you need to make your critics irrelevant. Over the years, I have seen many people who were can-do individuals, yet they listened to their critics instead of those who believed in them more than they believed in themselves. It derailed their dreams, their goals, and, for some, their future."

"I wouldn't know what to tell my friends," Anthony said.

"Don't focus on them; make them irrelevant to your life. If you really want them to know why you are coming here, why don't you just tell them the truth and move on?" I asked.

"They're going to think it's dumb," he said.

"You are putting too much concern on them. They can think it's dumb, and that's okay. Don't try and convince your critics. Stop seeking their approval, because the reality is, you will likely never win their approval. Mourn your loss and press ahead toward your goals. Your critics will face their own demise because of their consistent negative attitudes, and they pull down everyone around them."

"I just don't know if I can do this on my own."

I could see that Anthony didn't really have the support system that most people did. Even though his friends were a negative part of his life, they were still a reliable part, and that was something he didn't want to let go of.

I knew he could do this.

"You are destined for greatness, and you cannot allow the negative people in your life to pull you off track. The more you make progress toward your goals, the more resistance you may face from those critics around you."

"What if they try to prevent me from coming here?" he asked.

"They can do nothing to you without your permission. Even when they talk bad about you to others, do not allow this to stress you out. Keep doing what you know you are called to do. The credibility of your critics will be exposed in time as to who they really are. People around you probably know what your friends are like, so they have little credibility anyway. When you feel the presence of your critics, learn from them. Reflect on their behavior so that you never fall into that negative and destructive behavior."

"Is it possible that some of my friends will want to stick by me during this process?" Anthony asked.

"Of course," I assured him. "There is greatness in everyone. The relevant people whom you should align yourself with are the people that are encouraging you, the people who see something great within you. Real supporters may not always agree with you, but they will always support the decision you make and offer you their counsel. On the other hand, they will never try to control or manipulate your path in life."

Anthony was probably thinking a million things at that moment. I was asking him to step away from the things he'd known for years and follow me to something greater. I knew he had doubts that he could do it.

"I feel like I'm worried to tell my friends because they won't accept it. I want to do this, though. I'm hoping I am ready for it. If it's worked for Lalo, it could work for me."

"Then tell them that. If they can't be happy for you or see your progress, then it will be easier to break away from their dead-end lifestyles. The closer you are to accomplishing your goals, the more resistance you will face in your life. You must anticipate this and not allow it to shake you. When the going gets tough, understand that your ability to navigate through these challenging times is where you will grow and learn the most. It will develop your perseverance and increase your wisdom as a developing leader. Every challenge you encounter is by design, so allow it to be a mentoring moment rather than allow it to become a stressor.

"Anthony, let me share a little story about letting go that might help you understand. In Asia, monkeys are a delicacy. To catch the monkey, the hunter chains a wooden box with a small hole in the front to a tree. The hunter places fruits and nuts inside of the box. The monkey comes along and smells the fruits and nuts and is barely able to stretch his hand inside the box through the little hole to grab hold of the fruits and nuts. Now with his hand gripping the fruits and nuts, the monkey is unable to pull his hand back out because of his clenched fist. The monkey has trapped himself. If the monkey would simply let go of the fruits and nuts, he would free himself. However, the monkey can only think about that short-term win of having the fruits and nuts in his control and grip. Think about it; the monkey has now trapped himself and cannot even enjoy the very items that lured him into the trap in the first place. The monkey will scream, cry, even injure his wrist trying desperately to pull his hand out. The common-sense approach would be for the monkey to simply let go of the fruits and nuts and pull his hand out from the trap, freeing himself. Yet the monkey will not do it—will not let go. The monkey is his own worst enemy. In the same way, you are trapping yourself by not letting go of the old friends. If you let go, you will be released from their grip. It is all in your hands, Anthony."

"Kevin, I will make the change in my life. I'm ready for something greater to happen to me—away from the street life. Where do you think we should start?" he asked.

"I think we should work on getting you back into school."

Anthony seemed optimistic, but I could understand that it was a lot to take in at first.

"Kevin, I do want to go back to school and get a college degree. I just don't know if I would be able to."

"Anthony, of course you can. You are capable of doing anything that you put your mind to. Just remember I am there for you every step of the way. I would never set you up for failure."

"How do I know you will always be there for me?" he asked.

"Because we will trust each other," I said.

"How can you trust someone like me? I haven't exactly led the best life. I've made a lot of bad decisions."

It was easy for me to see that Anthony didn't see himself as worthy enough for the process. I knew I had to open up to him more.

"Let me tell you one last story about me and Lalo. One time I went to the movies with him during his mentoring process. He was about fifteen at the time. This was also when he was in a really bad place in his life. I told him I would save us two seats in the theater, and he could get us popcorn. I gave him my wallet, which had everything in it—my money, my ID, my credit cards, my cash, and my police identification card."

Anthony interrupted me. "Weren't you scared he would take your wallet and disappear?"

"There's a risk in every choice we make. He was already taking the biggest risk of trusting me that this process would work. I now trusted him to follow it through. It will be the same way with us, Anthony. We will grow from each other. For Lalo, it was a test to see if he could avoid temptation. For us, it might be something different."

Anthony seemed speechless. "I don't know what to say. It all seems unreal."

I couldn't help but laugh. I believe that each of us has a divine purpose in this world. I have seen amazing individuals accomplish great things in their lives. I have also watched them as they navigate through their journeys while encountering people who create barriers for them.

"I know, Anthony. I get that all the time."

Months later, I shared with Anthony something Lalo had written about his experience with PowerMentor.

> You think I can't relate with you? You think I don't know what you have been through? Gangs destroyed my life for many years. PowerMentor has been an incredible lifeline for me. My experience in high school back in the early 1990s was problematic, getting involved in fights and lacking

the drive, the support, and maybe even the willingness to really get into my education for my own benefit.

It kind of felt like I didn't have the actual competence to learn or the framework that could help provide the guidance I needed. With the peer distraction and the negative influences, I was set up to fail. In hindsight, if I had someone like a supportive parent or something on that level, it could have been a little bit easier to face those challenges.

Looking back, I didn't really have the parental support but instead had PowerMentor having an influence in my life that mitigated my wanting to give up. The mentors' involvement catapulted me to continue, and it gave me the encouragement to stay the course.

Unfortunately, during my high school years, I resisted the advice from PowerMentor, thinking I could have one foot in the good life and keep one foot in the bad life. I failed and was incarcerated, resulting in much of my education occurring within the justice system. I completed my high school diploma in juvenile hall in San Diego.

From home, I essentially only had my mom occasionally saying you need to finish your education. I really had no support at home. The only other support I had was my mentors, who always did whatever they could to assist me and wanted to kind of give me a leg up in education. I remember receiving an award for perfect attendance for approximately seven months that I had not missed even a single day of school.

It was helpful to see that PowerMentor would recognize something positive that I accomplished, and I know my mom appreciated that too.

My mother did do something special for me to motivate me to stay in school. Especially with having a single mom raising five kids, it was obviously challenging for her. Every morning she would give me a school allowance of five dollars to pay for my bus and for my lunch. It was an added incentive for me; however, at first, it really didn't work because it didn't influence me much. Later, I began recognizing the sacrifices my mother was making on my behalf for my education.

Initially in college, after incarceration for a number of years, I wanted to use that time to better my circumstances as much as possible for when I would be returning to the outside world for my future, my family, and the family that I would one day hope to have.

I greatly appreciated the PowerMentor program for their support system to encourage me and even to help me, because there were times in college where I felt below average. I was very much behind, because most of my education was in institutions for secondary schools. I was so grateful for the support that I had through my mentor Kevin, because he never stopped encouraging me and equipping and empowering me to finally succeed in earning my bachelor's, master's degree, and, currently, my doctorate.

The difficult transition being in college when you are in an institution is that the time is very limited, and sometimes there is difficulty making it to classes. So now you've got to juggle the time and your load of work with the missing opportunities to even get in front of the teacher.

I didn't have much outside research I could do. I essentially only had the books that were given to me by the professor and research papers that he would give to us. As far as the library or the Internet or other maybe family members that understood those bits of educational subjects, I really didn't have any of that, so it was extremely difficult for me.

I would have loved to have better resources to get caught up in the fundamentals of English or history or any of these subjects. I would have definitely appreciated that. It's hard to say what would have happened had I not had the PowerMentor program, because from my vantage point, I lagged on positive enthusiasm and support and just that encouragement they provided allowed me to want to continue to do more.

There are a number of obstacles that Latino males are going to run through if they are like me and they are in a single-parent home. Because the parents are usually lacking in the home because of trying to provide for the home, the individuals kind of run an independent program and they are a little bit carefree. I think the success of a mentor in that role to help fulfill the assistance you would get from parental support or even family support that is lacking—that would be a huge encouragement. That is probably what has made PowerMentor so successful.

It would give them an optimism personally to want to accomplish those goals and to obviously really drive home to that community to understand and recognize that it's education, maybe single-handedly, more than anything, that opens the doors for upper grade and greater opportunities. And that's whether it's law, business, medicine, or education—any of those. If they don't do it now, they don't consider the long-term, there can be devastating consequences and it's hard to pick yourself up in the future.

The education is what builds their understanding of the world that frames their outlook on life. It is the key that opens the doors to their dreams and ambitions. For them, I would say that I really try to frame in the sense that they would recognize and see that education is almost a must for their success. Also, to get them to own that understanding and most who are in my circumstance, the revolving door of staying in a poverty-stricken environment is extremely hard to break out of.

I like to ask people if they would want to stay in their environment and live like their parents or live like their friends in a poverty-stricken environment. Most would say no. I tell them that this is their almost golden ticket to get out of that environment. This helps them to make a better future for themselves and for others. I attempt to communicate that.

It's easier to drop out. It's easy to give up. It's more difficult to stay up late at night and open the books and read and study and read and do your work. It's very difficult to do that. It's the harder road, so it's easier to just kind of give in to your environment whether it's peer pressure or gangs or drugs or lack of support or poverty or any of these types of excuses. It's easier to fall into those traps and plug yourself into a role working at a minimum-wage job. You are given that routine.

The other reason, like in my case, I was the very first one to graduate high school. Because none of my cousins, my siblings, or my family members had graduated high school, or my parents for that matter, it was easier for me to not persevere and push myself to want to complete my education. It was just easier because it's natural not to do it in one respect. I think for many people, if you don't have your family members that have continued education, there is not really a drive for yourself to continue or complete it.

Things move very quickly, and if you are involved in gangs, then that's a huge encouragement to not continue high school. Drugs are a huge hurdle to overcome. If you are using drugs, you definitely don't have time to study. You are not going to spend five hours studying every night during the week. You are going to be off with the wrong crowd, and that crowd is susceptible to not completing their education so there are a number of these types of hurdles that they have to overcome.

I think without having a mentor, you kind of become what your peers are or what your peers tell you that you are, and you are in that kind of bottleneck trap and you are just kind of floating in life. You don't really have a direction or a purpose because nobody, no one, is attempting to encourage you to do the things that are beneficial for yourself. It's kind of a destructive pattern that you are in without a mentor.

Having a mentor is kind of like having an intact family, and I've never had an intact family but it is enlightening to envision one with a father and a mother really encouraging you to accomplish goals that are beneficial for you and your family. And so that's, I think, what the mentor's role did for me. It was a huge support system that I could always count on whether I was doing things right or doing things wrong.

The PowerMentor program was always there for me, and the individuals always saw the best in me. It didn't matter really what circumstances or what actions I was involved in. They were someone I could depend on, but they were also those who attempted to push me toward those hard things in life like getting an education, like wanting me to even help other people. Those were positives that came from that mentoring relationship.

I think having a support system, the analogy is the family, because it's always there and you recognize that it's there to equip you and benefit you and assist you that was extremely strong and to have somebody even to converse with. If I had a father, this is how I would envision it. You have a father there that you could say, "Well, how do I accomplish this in life?" Or, "How do I do that in life?" And the mentor role being there to give you those answers, provide that encouragement and support—that was, for me, a great strength.

I would go so far as to say that because of PowerMentor, that was extremely helpful in making me the man I am today by probably number one, always sticking with me even through those decisions I made that were leading me into a negative lifestyle. No matter what, my mentors were always a steady influence for me. Even when I kind of plateaued in my life and made poor decisions whether to skip out on education or wanting to go back to a negative influence in my peers into the gang scene, they believed in me and had a way of nurturing me back to greatness.

The mentors always pushed me out of that and encouraged me to want more and have a stronger desire and recognize those positive dreams and visions that I had for myself, then being attainable and pushing me toward attaining those goals, even when I didn't want to myself. It happened repeatedly, so many times, that it gave me great strength and confidence to want to push myself further from not only just getting a high school diploma but also getting a bachelor's degree. The mentors always believed that I could do more in these areas and never gave up provoking me in this direction so I would be able to even complete even my master's degree, work toward my doctorate, and finally begin speaking internationally about my life and how I overcame such adversity.

I remember initially some of the things that drew me to the PowerMentor program were the positive environment and how we had icebreaker activities. We would have events where we would go out and have a meal together, and we didn't have meals together at my home. It was kind of an experience to actually have to sit at a table at a restaurant with a mentor and talk through issues and on a basic level even understand the fundamentals of eating properly, sitting properly at a table, and using the right utensils.

All these things were learning experiences. I didn't experience these at home, so the mentor allowed me to learn these things, to not take them for granted but understanding that these are fundamentals for life and the benefit of learning these things. Also, going on different field trips with diverse learning opportunities, and again, it was a learning curve for me.

Going on a fishing trip with other peers and mentors and seeing the relationship there and being out in what I would call a neutral environment, being able to be more of yourself because you trusted the mentor and even learning the basics of fishing. Like what it is to cast the line and hook a fish and unhook a fish and all of these. These were things I never knew. In my environment, it probably would have been a long time before I ever went on these types of adventures.

Also, being able to really open your heart up because you trusted the mentor that you could share anything that you had in your heart or mind because, again, from my vantage point, you couldn't do that with your parents. I had no father at home, so I didn't have that person to share my life and my heart and my thoughts with.

My mother was very busy, and in my case, she was always tending to the younger children—my younger brothers and sisters. From that vantage point, it was extremely positive to have somebody that I could learn from and somebody that would direct me in my thoughts and in my ideas.

This all extremely increased my likelihood of graduating college by providing physical resources like books. Resources like if I had a question in my education, they would always assist me with answers or know what resource to provide for me but also the other resources, which I think might be even bigger resources. The commitment to push me personally with my ideas emotionally and mentally that I could really accomplish this because in myself I really didn't think I could do it.

I didn't think I was smart enough. I thought this was for another subset of people, but because of my background, I just kind of had given up. They would almost provide a barrier for me not to give up. The motivation to continue to thrive and to believe in me more than I believed in myself brought great strength that I gained from the mentors.

I thought a lot of things, but from my circumstances, without a mentor, I am certain I would never have succeeded. I would not have had the opportunity. I wouldn't know how to channel my emotions and my thoughts properly without a mentor. I would have been a statistic like everybody else, because my friends and my peers were making me out to be what they wanted me to be at my own expense and my own peril. PowerMentor instead brought out the best in me.

Without the mentor, I don't think that I would be standing here today, and in my circumstance, I probably would have never gotten out of prison. I would never have been able to help my family. I probably would not have graduated high school, college, or began my doctoral studies.

I might just add that we live in a society where three-quarters of the next generation have no male heads in their home. The whole aspect of positive reinforcement because of the negative environments that a lot of people live in is so far lacking that without mentors to stand shoulder to shoulder with this next generation, we will see a continued revolving door of imprisonment, drugs, gangs, and destructive lifestyles.

I think it is absolutely vital that more men and women stand up and decide to make a difference in their communities by helping the vulnerable, the young next generation, the students who may have a wish to do positive things in their lives but because of the circumstances that they have, may not have that opportunity without a mentor reaching out to them.

After I finished sharing what Lalo had written with Anthony, I turned to Anthony and said, "Anthony, you have a lot to be thankful for because you do not have kids or a family to take care of. Let me share with you about a young man who has had to try to change his life and go to college while trying to raise a family with a wife and three kids. Let me introduce you to Miguel."

After the introductions were made, Miguel began to speak. "Anthony, it's nice to meet you. My name is Miguel. I hope what I am going to share with you helps you take advantage of what you have, because I would have given anything to have a mentor come into my life before I had my first child at age seventeen. During my high-school years, I was mostly into sports. I was a pretty good student. The only thing that probably held me down was most of the ESL classes and other courses that I had; well, they would dumb things down for Hispanic or English-as-a-second-language students. The classes were set up to just occupy our time but not to actually help us learn.

"Obviously, the language was a barrier. They would just classify you and obviously stick you into courses that maybe didn't push you or didn't bring out the best in you by just giving you the basic literature dumbed down, or, I would say, something that is just basic. The way I see it is just so they could fill up a classroom compared to other classrooms that some of my friends were in where they required a lot from you. The teachers would have a little intellectual conversation with the students. It would create that atmosphere to where the student feels like they're learning, and they get to express their knowledge.

"Being in some of those classes really frustrated me, because the teachers wouldn't care. Obviously, they were just there to give me a grade and either pass me or fail me. The experiences that I faced in those classes where they didn't care what the outcome was with the student. Obviously, those classes were really simple, so my grades were As and Bs. I was really good in math, so math was probably the only subject where I got the chance to show the knowledge that I had.

"My goal during high school was to be a civil engineer. I based that on my fondness of math. Math was the subject that I really, really enjoyed. Going to college or maybe even a university was something on my top priorities. The downside of that was at that point I didn't have legal status in the United States. Although my goal was to go to college, I knew as soon as I graduated, those doors were going to get shut due to my illegal status.

"If I had the hope for college, it would have motivated me to keep on going to school and motivated me to stay out of trouble. Better still, to seek other things that made up my life during that period of time, which was sports or hanging out with the wrong people or influence or partying or that kind of lifestyle.

"I would say my family wasn't very involved with my education based of the language barrier, so anytime we had an open house or anything regarding school, they wouldn't attend for the same reason. They wouldn't understand what they were talking about. They had expectations for me to graduate high school. I think for most Latino parents, just graduating from high school is a big step. Then afterward, if they sought either college or going to a university, it's something way beyond their expectations.

"My parents, they wanted me to go to college, but they understood that money was an issue, and obviously, maybe illegal status also was an issue. I think my parents were just satisfied that I graduated from high school.

"A mentor or someone who would break it down for me and show me the ropes and say, 'Hey, I know you have this obstacle in your way, but there's other ways of going about it,' and showing me the ways so that I could go to college—wow, I would have taken advantage of that. Anthony, you have that advantage, but I did not.

"In my high school, there were a lot of mentors, but I think for some reason, it's just like scouting. They scout for those kids that already are doing good. The kids that were doing good, they would latch onto them. So that whenever they do become someone, they could claim a little, where they'll say, 'Hey, it's because of me that he made it.'

"It's just a little frustrating, because you could tell the students who actually needed the extra help and those who already had parents who were wealthy or those who had parents who understood the language. And so for those who didn't have that, it felt like a big disadvantage, and I lost motivation.

"Based on what my experiences were, it was as if you would educate the parents or try to get the parents more involved in the child's education; that would probably make them understand that we as Hispanics have more potential than just graduating from high school. The most important thing is just, I guess, the Hispanic male—a place or role to where as soon as they get a certain age, they have to provide for the family.

"I think that's why most Hispanic males dropped out of high school. They have to fulfill that role that the parents have set aside for them. So maybe it would be better to get to the parents and make them understand that even though it's his duty as a Hispanic male to take care of the family, it would be wiser in the long run if he continues his education. That way, he can provide better in the future rather than right after high school.

"I think they're not seeing it because they get to a certain age, and when they see them just either hanging out and doing something bad, I don't know, I feel that they think, 'Hey, he's better off working than going to school.' They want to see the short-term benefits out of it than rather than long-term benefits.

"Anthony, as you are well aware, Latinos get negative peer pressure when they talk about liking school. I think they would definitely experience a lot of negative pressure from the parents, because, like I said, their parents want them to do something else. I don't know. It's difficult in a sense, because not only do they have their parents on one side putting in negative pressure. They also are hanging around the wrong people whose lives are influenced by either gangs or negative activity, and then they're going to be drawn to that side rather than education. It's got to be a balance of family and the people they're surrounded by. Anthony, you have to choose one or the other, because if you do not, it will be chosen for you, and you will have missed this once-in-a-lifetime opportunity to have someone come alongside of you and walk you through the tough times to get to your future.

"I mentioned before—the people they hang around with, whether it's a negative influence or even a positive influence. Guys who get to a certain age either get frustrated or, like in my case, probably frustrated of putting the work in to see a good outcome later on in the future rather than right away. It's just matter of being patient and putting in the work to get something good out of it.

"I would definitely think it would change drastically because me, personally, I think I have a lot of potential. Like I said, I was really good in math. I think by having a mentor, it would have changed the outcome of my life by staying focused. I would definitely have sought my goal of being in civil engineering. If not that, something where I know I would make my family proud. I really think a mentor would do a lot of guys good just to keep them focused and aligned with what their goals are. Anthony, don't miss this!

"I think some of my greatest barriers were just hanging out with the wrong people and being influenced. Maybe being too naïve was what was really going on and thinking that I could make it happen, and in reality, I was just digging myself into a hole and later on wouldn't be able to dig myself out of it. I was putting other priorities before education.

"The competing priorities were just, I would say, being popular and already establishing a short-term future for myself. Yet, I knew that I didn't have papers, so I had to do a plan B, knowing that wasn't the right way to go, but it was just forcing … maybe the option I had.

"Often, I realized I was my own worst enemy. The choices that I made were the greatest barrier. Growing up from a young man to a man and having a girlfriend who was pregnant and having to step up to that role of providing for them, not only did it take my focus off of education, I shifted that energy into something else. So that was one of the biggest obstacles preventing me from going to college. The way I focused my energy was not in the right direction. Anthony, you were smart enough to not have a kid early in life, so you, more than anyone, have a great opportunity to turn things around in your life. Do it now!

"I wasn't the type of person that was just giving up; it's knowing what I went through. The energy that I put into that—I know that if I would have put the same energy into college, it would have been something else, something different in such a great way.

"The only thing that I can think about is just Latinos are—I hate to say—really very easily influenced. We really need a voice and someone to push us in the right direction. The way I see it is the majority of the Latino males are lost, and they seek either popularity or they seek other areas where they feel their presence is valued, whether it's in a gang or whether it's getting a girl knocked up and becoming the father figure. That's basically what I went through.

"Anthony, I hope you really listen to what I have shared with you. In a few short years, you can be a decade ahead of where I am at right now. I would have given anything to be in the shoes you are in right now. You are smart and have all of the resources right in front of you, but you have to choose to put both feet in.

"Fortunately, I too was introduced to PowerMentor, and even though I had a family to be responsible for, I too now am attending the university to earn my bachelor's degree. However, I could have been so much further along if I would have learned this long before. You now have that choice, and I can tell you that the impact my mentor has had on my life is priceless, and I would not trade it for anything!"

Anthony was speechless as he reflected on all that he had been told. He had never heard such amazing stories, and this time, he was about to apply what the others experienced in their lives to what he was experiencing at the time.

CHAPTER THREE
Nothing Is Impossible

During our last meeting, Anthony and I had decided that school should be the top priority for him. I gave him some homework, asking him to put together his information so we could submit it to the local community college during registration.

Several months had passed, and I was excited to meet up with Anthony again. At our arranged time and place, I saw him come through the entrance. This time, Anthony was standing there alone.

"Hi, Anthony. What's up?" I asked.

"Not too much."

"No friends this week?"

"No, it's just me," he happily replied.

He pulled up a chair at our designated table, which had become our special place of connection and reflection. In a relatively short period of time, I could already see the change in Anthony. He was beginning to think much more critically and making decisions based on outcomes rather than impulse. He was beginning to believe that something truly great lay ahead in his future. Just the smallest steps had taken him so far.

"Anthony, that is awesome," I told him. "I'm so proud of your accomplishments in your journey toward your future."

"I really haven't done too much," he said.

"Anthony, you need to realize that every step is a great accomplishment. Every small step you take brings you closer to your goal. I can tell that this process means a lot to you, because it took courage and determination to stand up to your friends. If you didn't have that, then you could constantly be persuaded to go back to your old life."

It was inspiring to see how much Anthony's attitude had changed within just a few months.

The barista at the Starbucks stopped by our table as he mopped the floor and asked us how we were doing. Our frequent meetings had allowed us to become acquainted with many of the staff.

"I think I'm already able to see the difference," Anthony said.

"In what way?" I challenged him.

"My friends always talk about things they would like to do. I've been talking about things I'm going to do," he told me.

"Think about how much you have done so far. You said yes to changing your life, you said yes to this journey, and now you're saying yes to finding the type of friends who will encourage and inspire you."

I had to make sure that Anthony didn't doubt his progress. I had to be the one to keep him focused and on track with a proper perspective of this transformation. I understood that it could be tough at times.

"Kevin, if it weren't for you, I don't know if I would be able to do this."

"It's all within you, Anthony. But that is also why I am here—to help you to your path. How has your week been?"

"It's been okay," he said. "I use my path to keep me focused and on the right path. When I felt like my friends were trying to pull me the wrong way, I told them about how I was forming this application for school."

"Anthony, that is amazing. How did they respond?"

"My friend whom I have the felony with asked how I could succeed with everything that has happened. He said graduating from school would be great but would be really tough for me. He kind of got me thinking that I was in over my head. He said maybe I could wait until we could do it together."

I knew Anthony would encounter this type of problem. That's why I thought it was so important to meet up with him whenever he wanted, especially in the beginning. He was surrounded by more people who didn't know the right path than ones who did.

"Anthony, this guy is going to be your toughest critic. He's the closest to you and is the most similar to you."

"Don't you think he has a good point?" Anthony asked. "He might just be looking out for me."

"No. Some critics are not so obvious. Someone like him is a passive-aggressive critic. These are people who have convinced themselves that they are actually helping you by being your critic. This is the person who makes comments like, 'Are you okay? You look sick today.' They always point out the negative but then try and convince you that they have your best interest at heart. This is the furthest thing from the truth."

"So you think he might still be holding me back?"

"Absolutely. When you tell a passive-aggressive critic your dream of becoming a lawyer, he will say something like, 'Are you sure, because that's a lot of schooling, and I can't see you doing that.' This is very different from a friend who is trying to help you make a decision objectively by discussing the pros and cons."

"How can you tell the difference?"

"Once it becomes personal, they will reveal their motives. As soon as they personalize it, you know they are not in your corner. When you let your friend know you will continue with school and he is more than welcome to join you, do not expect his support. Shake him off and keep him at a distance, because he will likely be a discouragement for you."

"I'm going to tell him that I am strong enough to make it," Anthony said.

"Anthony, that is the perfect response," I noted. "You have the ability to take what is meant by others to harm you and use it for your advantage. How you react to things is far more important for you than the circumstances of what happened to you. Now, if he is your true friend, he will support you on your path. Maybe even one day, you can inspire him to find the right path too."

I then formally invited Anthony to begin attending regular meetings with others within PowerMentor so that he could see their progress and newfound purpose in their lives. Anthony said he would probably feel a little uncomfortable at first; however, he felt he would soon develop solid friendships with many who were just ahead of him in their college journeys.

"I feel a lot more confident now than I did when I walked in through that door today," he said.

"Anthony, that is great. Did you also bring all the information that I needed to complete the college application and put together your first résumé?"

Anthony reached into his backpack and pulled out a notebook that had scribbles of information written down on it.

"Anthony, this is all great. Thank you. Your college application is really coming together. Now that we have most of the information that I need, can you tell me of any other clubs, activities, sports, or interests you had outside of high school?"

"No, I don't think so. I didn't play sports in high school, and I didn't belong to any clubs. I struggled just to go to my classes."

"Have you worked at any place other than Einstein Bros?"

"No, that's been my only job."

There was a silence between us as I was trying to think about what to put on the résumé other than his current job and his high school.

"What is it? You look like you're really thinking hard," he finally said.

"Just trying to figure out some other things to fill your résumé with."

Anthony seemed frustrated. "I can't do this. I am up against so much. From where I was raised and my background, it won't get me anywhere."

"Anthony, I have known many people who were up against more than you are."

"That can't be possible."

"Of course it's possible. Completing the résumé is just a small step in your journey. Many guys I started mentoring had many more obstacles than this."

"Maybe I should just work more until I'm ready for a better résumé."

"That won't be necessary, Anthony. Remember Jose Orozco whom I told you about? Maybe I should just tell you more about his story and all he had endured. Now this guy makes your felony conviction look like a cakewalk. Interestingly, Anthony, I met Jose almost the same way I met you. Jose was also working at a fast-food restaurant.

"I met a then eighteen-year-old Jose many times in 1998. At the time,

I was serving my last term as the president of the Grossmont Union High School District Governing Board in San Diego's East County.

"As president, I was responsible for planning the agenda, conducting meetings, and balancing the budget. The school district served more than twenty-two thousand students and had an annual budget of $210 million. I was responsible for bringing financial accountability to a district that was facing major long-term debt.

"Also, at the time, I was still in my midtwenties. I had no college education or college experience. It was an honor to serve and something I took very seriously; yet, at times, I felt in over my head.

"This position meant a great deal to me, because I won the election in a landslide victory. It was clear that the community saw something in me. I could bring change and stability to the school system. However, I felt I was in over my head. I was in my midtwenties and had never experienced a leadership role such as this. I was scared and wondered how I would navigate through all of the politics. Each side would lobby me for what they hoped I would accomplish during my tenure. The competing interests were so complex. In a similar way, your friends and the new friends you are making have competing interests. As it was critical for me to discern each side's interest, it is also critical for your success.

"On the way home one day, I stopped in the drive-through of the local a Jack in the Box restaurant.

"'Welcome to Jack in the Box. How can I help you?' I heard unenthusiastically from the box.

"After placing my order, I arrived at the first window as instructed. I was met by the drive-through attendant who reminded me how much I owed. He had a harsh look to him. He had a completely shaved head with the exception of a tail in the back. He had eyes with a vaguely unsettling quality.

"We had to wait for my order, so we looked at each other in an awkward silence. His eyes looked right through me. There was something about him that I could not put my finger on. I decided to break the silence.

"As the founder of PowerMentor, I was used to reaching out to complete strangers. 'Can I ask you a question?' I asked him. He replied no, and I laughed. 'Well, I'm going to ask anyway,' I told him. 'You in college?' He frowned at me and shook his head.

"He went on to tell me that he had dropped out of high school. "He didn't have much of an interest to talk to me, but I kept pushing, asking him if he always worked so late at night. He explained that he did, because the third shift paid more. I continued to press him for information and discovered that he hadn't set out to work in the fast-food industry but felt like there was at least potential for a promotion and pay raise down the road.

"I asked him about college, but he seemed to shrug off my question as he handed me my bag of food. The restaurant was unusually slow that day, with few customers in sight, so I kept talking. I asked him to think back to his childhood and asked what he had wanted to be when he grew up. He smiled at me and answered that he'd always thought he would be an attorney. He followed up his statement with, 'I know it's stupid.'

"Even though I had the sandwich in the car, I was compelled to stay and hear the rest of his story, especially considering there were no cars behind me. I told him that I didn't think it was stupid at all and added that I believed he could go back to school and become an attorney. 'It's all up to you,' I told him.

"Jose thanked me before wishing me a good night and telling me to come back again. Then he shut the drive-through window, and off I went.

"I thought a lot about my interaction with Jose. I had taken a break from mentoring at-risk young people because, at times, it became very emotionally draining. It became discouraging when those I'd invested in continued to make poor decisions or, worse yet, life was snatched from them by senseless street violence. When I felt myself putting in less than 100 percent, I stepped away. Mentoring is serious business, and it is better to not mentor at all if you cannot commit to it 100 percent. And so, I was conflicted about whether I should push this guy to go back to school.

"After a few days, I decided to return to the restaurant, simply because I was now hooked on that Croissan'wich. I found myself crossing paths with the mysterious drive-through attendant again. He said that he remembered me from before and quickly offered me a smile.

"I asked him what had made him remember. He laughed a little, and I felt that rough exterior from before begin to slowly fade. He went on to explain that it had been a long time since anyone had asked him about his future goals. But it was more than just that, he noted. He said it was that I had told him that he could actually do something that he could not picture himself.

"It was at that point that I noticed his nametag, which said Jose on it. I then asked him, by name, if he had thought about what we had talked about the last time. Chuckling, he admitted he had. A relationship was coming to fruition. Yet, I did not fully recognize the implication of this newfound connection with Jose."

"Just like the connection you said you experienced with me," Anthony said.

"Yes, Anthony. It was just like that. It was the connection that doesn't always happen. It's the moment when you meet someone who is meant to do great things but they haven't reached that potential yet," I confirmed.

"Jose worked at a restaurant just like me. He saw himself there, because he didn't feel like he could go anywhere else. He needed that encouragement to get him to where he needed to go."

"Exactly. I decided at that moment that Jose could make that change, and I resolved to try as hard as I could to help Jose achieve his dream. Maybe it was for the best I had stepped away from mentoring when I did. It gave me the time to step back and approach each situation with a different perspective. I put it in God's hands, and He led me straight to Jose. Many tell me that I have a unique gift to inspire those whom most see as misfits. At times, it feels as though this is too great a responsibility. There is too much at stake if it is not done right, and the easy way out is to simply shirk that responsibility. Yet, deep down, I knew that I had a special calling in my life. Many would tell me, 'Kevin, everyone you take the time to seriously mentor completely changes his life. Do you understand how unique that is?'

"I often do not like to share stories of things that happen during my day-to-day encounters with people. Quite frankly, unless one were to walk alongside of me, much of it does not seem possible. Yet, these things happen, and those who do walk by my side see the amazing things that occur. For example, I can feel led to encourage someone whom I do not know very well, and often, after I give him some encouraging words, he begins to cry and thank me for giving him hope. It is something that at times I cannot even explain because it is at such a depth that is difficult to put into words.

"On one occasion, I picked up a packet from the San Diego City Schools GED program and dropped it off for Jose at Jack in the Box. He asked me what it was, and I explained that it was everything he needed to complete the GED program and finish high school. He looked at me like I was joking with it when I suggested we get started right away."

I paused my story and looked across at Anthony for a long moment. He seemed troubled, and I understood why. He was trying to make the right decisions in life, which wasn't always easy.

"Let me tell you more about Jose." And so, I told him more about Jose and how he'd inspired me to make positive changes in my own life.

"But Jose didn't have a felony record like I did," he said.

"Well, let me continue with what Jose was faced with," I explained.

I then recounted the following story to Anthony:

A few weeks had gone by when some friends and I decided to go on a hiking trip to Cedar Creek Falls. This was a beautiful place to hike for the day with a waterfall that we could rappel down; it was an adventure. The trails there offered an exquisite view of San Diego away from the traffic, the buildings, and the people. In all, it was six miles of birds, trees, and a waterfall.

We decided to stop at Jack in the Box before hitting the road. Upon entering, we were greeted by a smiling Jose.

"How's the studying going?" I asked.

"It's coming along. Working a lot, so I study when I can," he replied.

Jose looked past me to see my vehicle sitting in the parking lot. It was secured with climbing gear and equipment on the top cargo rack.

"What are you up to today?" Jose asked.

"We are heading up to Cedar Creek Falls to hike with some friends," I said.

"That sounds exciting. I've never been to Cedar Creek Falls before. I've actually never been hiking at all."

"Really?" I asked. "It's a fun time. Great for exercise and getting outside."

Jose took a second to muster up what he wanted to say. "My shift is over in a few minutes. Would you mind waiting so I can go with you guys? If you don't mind and have the room."

I was kind of surprised. I really didn't know him too well. Because I wanted him to do better in his life and was showing him a path toward his GED, I thought maybe this would be a good time to find a deeper connection.

"Sure, let's go!" was all I could hear myself say.

After arriving at Cedar Creek Falls, I decided to take my time getting to know Jose. We started along the hike and began sharing with each other our philosophies of life. We talked about what we each felt was the purpose in life and why we were in this world. I opened up about the challenges I had experienced in my life. I had a tough time in school and struggled with ADHD.

As we talked and paused several times on our hike, we fell back from the group, as we were steeped in deep discussion. I expressed how I wished someone had come alongside me and believed in me. A lot of my struggles were my own personal struggles and issues I had to deal with alone. It would have been nice if someone believed in me and helped me to become the person I was created to be. My purpose in life was to be for others what I wish I'd had in my life.

Jose spoke about how he wasn't sure what he believed in. We talked about religion, and he asked if I believe in God.

I said, "Yes. I have a strong foundation of core values. My belief in God is the strongest asset that I have."

He said he wasn't sure, because in school they told him there was no such thing. I couldn't believe that a school establishment would teach him something like that. It was just another example of how our upbringings were very different from one another.

I explained to him that I had a deep personal relationship with God. If it weren't for God, I wouldn't have been able to get through some tough times. God had also helped me on my path and brought me to some incredible people, such as Jose himself. I was pretty confident God was real.

I could see that Jose was a deep thinker. He was able to draw me into seeing things from a completely different perspective. I told Jose that if he had any doubts about himself to turn to God. He would challenge me about my beliefs such as how I knew God was real.

I soon realized that even though I was leading and mentoring him, I could feel him leading and mentoring me simultaneously. He challenged and questioned a lot of things I said. He was searching for a deeper meaning. Even though on some aspects we had different viewpoints, it was the intellectual conversation that I admired the most.

Jose was a great individual. I knew I would learn a great deal from him. He would be able to impact my life so much that I would never be the same.

When I was done recounting that day with Jose, Anthony chimed in. "Jose seemed very smart. Better than a shift leader at a fast-food restaurant. He could have really been an attorney."

"Yes, I'm glad you see it from him now, because I did too," I told him.

"So what happened between becoming an attorney and dropping out of high school?" he asked.

"During our hike, Jose shared with me how hard of a life he had already led. He grew up in Logan Heights, a very rough area of San Diego. He didn't grow up with money, but his parents made sure they had what they needed to get by. He was very close to his mother and spoke about her in the most endearing way. His fondest memories of his childhood with her included her delicious food and the stories she would read him before he went to bed. Unfortunately, Jose's mother died of cancer when he was only eight years old.

"The responsibility of raising Jose rested on his father. He was a very strict man who expected a lot out of Jose. Because he worked a lot, Jose's father relied on close family members and friends to help Jose and give him a womanly figure in his life. Cancer was unkind of Jose again, as it would also claim the life of his father. When his father passed away, Jose was just twelve.

"You were right," Anthony said. "Jose endured much more than me from such a young age. I still have all of my family members and friends."

"It was tough, Anthony. You look up to people for guidance and support, and when they are taken away from you, it's hard to find the right path.

"Jose then found himself on his own, bouncing from family member to family member. Even though he had a place to rest his head every night, he never was able to find a home. His parents couldn't be replaced.

"Jose told me that when he was sixteen, he dropped out of school. It was time for him to become an adult. He didn't have his mom or dad to help him with his homework, to teach him how to drive a car, or to pick out a suit for the prom. He couldn't think about becoming a lawyer. That was for kids with money. He didn't have that.

"He also said that he didn't want to be like so many kids who turn to the streets. Even though Jose had turned to the streets himself, he knew that was not what he wanted. He wanted to make a decent living for himself, so he started working fast-food jobs. It gave him the hours and the paycheck that he needed to survive on his own. The job that he had now was going to give him the stability and the opportunity to grow in the company.

"I could see where Jose was coming from in the realistic sense. He needed a career, and he had one. But Jose still needed to accept his fate. I once asked him if his passion to be an attorney had faded away with time. It hadn't.

"I wanted Jose to remember what we had talked about. Anything is possible. He needed to follow his dream. He was too scared to fail, but I was going to give him all the encouragement he needed. Failure was not going to be an option with us. When we got back that day, Jose was going to make a plan for when he was going to take his GED.

"Jose had one more thing to tell me. He didn't have legal status in the United States."

Anthony interrupted me right there. "What? He had no parents, no high-school diploma, and no citizenship?" he asked, wide eyed.

"Yes, that's right, Anthony. I'm telling you there are people much worse than your situation. If they can do it, you can do it."

"Did you ever think it was going to be too much for you?" Anthony asked.

"I knew it was going to be a long process. I knew it was going to take some long nights and some hard work. However, I never thought for a second that it couldn't be done. Jose was a smart guy. He was going to achieve his dream; I was convinced of that.

"After encouraging Jose, his life took off. There was something very different about Jose from that moment forward. I was forever grateful that I told him he could come along on the hiking trip. It was then that we formed a lifelong relationship that would never fade. It still continues to this day," I told Anthony.

"Does Jose's story stop there?" he asked.

"Oh, no! It had just begun. Jose went back to school using the packet I had originally dropped off for him. After some hard work and a lot of study time and determination, Jose obtained his GED. He then registered for San Diego City College. I could never be able to describe how proud I was of Jose for reaching so far. This was a two-year community college that would get him adjusted to college and give him the opportunity to work at the same time.

"It wasn't always going to be easy. In fact, most of the time it was quite difficult. But Jose was determined to stay focused on his goal.

"After completion at San Diego City College, he enrolled at San Diego State University. He sought a double major in philosophy and political science. After graduation, Jose then took the Law School Aptitude Test so that he could be accepted into law school.

"There was only one problem. For Jose to be accepted into law school, he had to have his citizenship papers, which we didn't have. All throughout college we held hope that he would receive his Certification of Citizenship. We would continue to contact immigration to find out if his papers had gone through, but we never got good news.

"Over and over again, Jose would be let down. At time, he would be drawn to tears. Feelings of hopelessness would arise from time to time as he felt he would never get his legal status in the United States. At times, I would reflect, *What if I am getting Jose's hopes up for nothing? What if we are not successful in obtaining his legal documents? What will I tell him, and how will he react?* Yet, deep down, I truly believed that it would happen. I mean, he had done his part, and now it was time for this to come to fruition. I would find myself praying constantly for God to reward Jose for his diligence. I would also reflect that at times I felt our journey was so intertwined that if I failed in my quest to complete college, it could impact Jose's journey, and vice versa. We would both have to do our part, while we would ask God to do His part.

"I would then feel more confident and encourage Jose and tell him how confident I was that it would come to pass at the right time. It was hard for me as well, because I wanted this for him so badly. I had to be strong and put my faith in God.

"Finally, during his last year at San Diego State University, Jose received his Certification of Citizenship. He was accepted into law school at California Western School of Law. All of his hard work had paid off, and I was truly blessed to attend his graduation."

"Kevin, I don't believe how this story can be true," Anthony said, still wide eyed.

"I know, Anthony. If I didn't experience it myself, I would be thinking the same thing. But do you see? This is going to be you—another unbelievable story of strength and determination!"

"Can I meet this guy? Jose?"

"Yes, Anthony, you will meet him!"

"I'm starting to believe that everything I want from life, I can get."

"That is great, Anthony! I knew it was in you. Let me also share one more thing with you before you leave."

I grabbed a piece of paper from my backpack. It was a speech that I had written based on my experiences. The week before, I'd had the honor of speaking at the California Western School of Law on the topic of mentorship and community service. It was incredible to share Jose's story with people who did not realize how far he had come along in his life. Jose also spoke at the law school.

"Anthony, these are Jose's actual words on what mentorship has meant to him. It reads: 'You only get a chance like this once in a lifetime. You buy tickets every week and then wait anxiously for the next day to see if you hit the jackpot. I didn't win the lottery that night, but I also didn't buy a lottery ticket either. In fact, I never bought one. That night, however, was my luckiest day.'"

As I read the words to Anthony, I thought about how that night I'd had a lump in my throat as I heard Jose refer to the day we met as the luckiest day of his life. I reflected on all that had transpired in both of our lives—our progress, our friendship, our experiences. I began to really grasp the gravity of what an amazing mentoring relationship we had been blessed with.

Jose's speech continued: "I was working at a Jack in the Box in North Park. I was fairly new on the job and was just getting the hang of things. While taking an order at the register, a group of people walked in. 'Big deal, huh?' Groups of people always walk into Jack in the Box.

Oh no, these were not just like any group of individuals. With them was a special person, one whom only God knew would change me forever."

Looking at Anthony, I could tell he has been inspired.

"I can do this, Kevin. If Jose can do it, I can do it," he said.

"I know you can, Anthony. Let's get back to that résumé. What do you say?"

— — —

Anthony and I continued to reflect on the fact that he was beginning to really believe that he could change his life forever. He was really impacted, and sharing Jose's story with him had rekindled emotions that lay deep within my heart for the amazing impact that I'd had on Jose and that Jose had on me.

"Anthony, it will be important for you to align yourself with friends who are also going to college and making a better life."

"Kevin, it is hard to relate with the people I see at college. They are not from where I am from, so it is awkward."

After several weeks had passed, Anthony and I continued to dialogue about who we surrounded ourselves with.

"Anthony, let me introduce you to a few guys who are on the journey the same as you. These guys can relate to you, and they are working, going to college, and resisting the negative influences. Let me introduce you to David Rios, Daniel Vasquez, and Alex Morales. In fact, you met Alex when we were working on the humanitarian project in Tecate, Mexico, a few weeks ago."

Anthony had embarked on his first humanitarian project with PowerMentor and came face to face with the reality that there were many people that are less fortunate that he was. He met kids who had been abandoned by their parents, and I could see how much it impacted Anthony even though he tried to maintain his tough exterior.

"Oh, yes," Anthony said. "I remember him. He was a good guy, and we had a lot of fun working on that together."

With that, David introduced himself and began to talk. "Anthony, it is great to meet you. My name is David, and I have known Kevin for more than twenty years. I met Kevin when I was fifteen years old and involved in his boxing program. I graduated high school, work hard as a carpenter and painter, and have a wife and three children. Anthony, what I would say is that you have it made right now. You do not have responsibilities to a wife and kids, so you have the unique opportunity to go to college and break the cycle of poverty in the Latino community. I hope you take it seriously. Over the years, we have seen guys do amazing things with their lives, and it all starts with a decision and a commitment to stay away from the negative influences. I have stood by Kevin for so long, and we have always helped each other whenever needed. That is what true friendship is. The guys you know from the neighborhood are corrupted in their type of friendship. It is conditional, and they themselves are lost, so it is like the blind leading the blind. Trust me, Anthony; it is no accident that your life is changing, and you will have the opportunity to do great things in your life and impact the world around you. We are there for you and will always stand by you and support you."

"Thank you for your words, David," Anthony said. "I really appreciate that. It is crazy how long you guys have all known each other and have been working together to help others. In twenty years, I want to be able to say the same thing."

"Anthony, my name is Daniel, and I have been involved in PowerMentor for a long time. My cousin is Jose Orozco, whom you know. I was able to see Jose's life change from one extreme to the other. I always stayed close to Jose and Kevin, because I could see there was something different about what they would tell me and how they would teach me to make better decisions. Sometimes I let the negative influences in my life drown out their voices, and I suffered as a result.

"I also tried to do for my younger brothers what Jose and Kevin did for me, but it was really hard. Last year one of my brothers was shot and killed by the police because he was driving a stolen car. When they tried to pull him over, he sped toward them, and they shot him. My youngest brother was in the backseat. He was not killed, but my other brother was. It was so hard, so painful. If I only could have done more to keep him out of trouble, but ultimately, it was his decision.

"I remember one week before this happened, Kevin and I were driving through City Heights, and we saw him. Kevin asked him, 'Jonathan, are you ready to make some changes in your life? Because the way you are going, you are headed for more trouble.' Jonathan shrugged it off and did not listen, and one week later, his life was no more—all because of his immaturity and poor decisions.

"Anthony, for your sake, I really hope you recognize the opportunity that is before you, because you may not get another chance at this!"

"Thank you, Daniel. I appreciate your words, and I am sorry for what happened to your brother. I knew of him, and yes, he made the wrong decisions. I think I am getting on the right track!"

"Alex," Anthony noted, "I remember when you and I helped Kevin with the project in Tecate, Mexico. That was awesome."

"Anthony, when we were in Tecate, Mexico, working on that orphanage, it really made me feel good about who I was and what we were doing," Alex said.

"Yes, Alex, I agree. I felt so much purpose in my life in helping other people. It was hard work, but it was a really great opportunity."

"You and I have a lot in common in that we both are trying to make it in this life and keep away from the negative influences," Alex continued. "I hope you really stick to this, because I look forward to us working together in the future. I have known Kevin for a long time, and what the other guys are telling you, I agree; this is a great opportunity for you. I know it is hard at times to let go of the friends who are not compatible with the desired changes you have made. I can see that you are really smart, and I just hope things go well."

Anthony expressed doubts about whether he could actually make it in school. Anthony also expressed concern that his criminal record could make all his efforts futile. The other guys offered encouragement to Anthony. Anthony clearly became emotional and shared his inner doubts, his feelings of despair, and his lack of hope for the future. The exchange between all of the guys was very moving. I knew it would surface again in the near future as Anthony would reflect on all that was discussed.

— — —

Sometimes it was hard for me to believe the progress Anthony was making. We were able to get a résumé together for him and send it out. He was quickly accepted to San Diego Community College, where he began taking classes. He still had his ups and downs, but he stayed focused and determined.

Anthony began to share his interest in going to law school. Yet, he also recognized the uphill battle to be accepted into law school with a felony conviction. I knew he was meant for greatness when he first expressed his interest in becoming a firefighter. He wanted to help people and serve his community. Being a lawyer was the perfect spot for him, yet I could not be certain we would be successful in expunging his conviction. Hearing the stories of the men who went before him had inspired him to achieve his dreams.

He also wanted the opportunity to defend people who needed advocacy. He wanted to stick up for guys who were just like him—guys who felt like they had no chance in life and people wouldn't fight for them.

His classes were going very well. He attended them because he had an interest in them. When he needed help with anything–homework, classes, or grades–he called me. I'd been there for him every step of the way for almost two years.

Anthony called and asked me if we could get something to eat for dinner. I agreed.

"Anthony, how are you?" I asked.

Even though we stayed in regular contact, it was nice to see him face-to-face. There's only so much you can say over the phone before you want to meet up in person. I also wanted to share with Anthony that it would be challenging working a full-time job while also going to college full-time. The cost of the books is very expensive. I explained to Anthony that because of his progress, I would pay for his books now. He was so happy because he knew how far he must stretch every dollar.

"I've been doing really well," he said. "I got my grades back and am getting ready for this next semester. My guidance counselor gave me this packet so I will know what I need to be accepted at San Diego State University."

"That's great! Can I see it?" I asked.

Anthony reached into his backpack and pulled out a packet. When he did, a sheet of paper escaped his grasp. I leaned over to pick it up and saw it was a math test that Anthony had performed poorly on.

"Anthony, what is this?" I asked.

Anthony became flustered. "It's nothing," he said.

"Do you need help with your studies?" I asked him.

"No, I'm fine. It's just one test."

"I understand it's one test. I just don't want this to be a reoccurring issue. Is this why it's taken us longer to get together this time?"

Anthony and I had been able to meet up with each other on a pretty regular basis. When I called and he wasn't quick to get back to me, I knew something had to be wrong. In the mentoring process, when your schedule becomes irregular, it's typically a sign of straying off the path. I didn't intend to bring it up to him, but I knew something was off.

"I know what you're going to say," he said. "I'm not that great at math, okay? A lot of people aren't."

"I agree with you, but there are things you can do to get the help.

Ask your teacher or ask me. There are probably office hours you can go to for tutoring. Maybe there's extra help sessions or tutors. You can raise this grade with no problem."

Anthony seemed frustrated. "That's easy for you to say. It's always been easy for you. You can just look at someone like me and help everyone else out. But you've never had to go through this process yourself. You've never had to be the one with the odds against you. I will always be the underdog. I could never be the one who inspires you to do great things."

"That's not true, Anthony. While working with Jose, he and I had an amazing connection. We just clicked. He did not realize it, but God was actually using him to shape my life more than ever. Jose thought I was there to mentor him, yet, in many ways, he was mentoring me. Jose impacted my life so much that he is one of the main individuals responsible for where I am today. I have come a long way since I started to mentor others. I have grown in such miraculous ways. I know none of it would have been possible without the people I've mentored pushing me to reach my goals."

I realized in that moment that despite our many conversations, I had never really opened up about what my life was like at his age.

"How?" he asked, pushing on.

"There are a lot of things about me that you still have to learn."

"Oh, yeah. Like what?"

"Anthony, I'm not perfect. I didn't come from the perfect family, as you might think I did. My father wasn't the positive role model I had hoped he would be. He wasn't there for me, didn't encourage me, and didn't walk alongside me in my life. I had to watch him treat my mother poorly and set a bad example for my siblings and me. I was fortunate enough to have an elderly neighbor who mentored me. It made me realize that I could give a positive experience to someone who was missing out on life, just like me. I have to remind myself that I've come far in my life, having grown up with a father who was not a positive role model or an encouraging influence." I sighed as memories of how he'd fight with my mom came rushing in.

"I never knew that about you," Anthony said. "What was your mentor like?"

"His name was Mr. Sylvester," I said. "I would see him from time to time working on his lawn. He would always wave to me and ask me how I was doing. He used to tell me how he could see something very special about me. It was nice to get that kind of attention from someone. He was a very positive influence."

"Did he help you out like you are helping me out?" Anthony asked.

"He never specifically told me that he would be there for me. He was there in his words more than his actions. He was the first person to point out my strengths and the first one to tell me if I was headed in the wrong direction."

"Was he just around when you were a kid?" he continued to ask.

"Actually, Mr. Sylvester was the most influential to me during my teenage years. He even went as far as to tell me what would help when I got acne for the first time."

"Did it make you angry that your dad was not there for you?"

I had to think about this question for a minute. My dad had become a good thing for me in a bad way. I had come to terms with how my relationship with my father had led to where I was as an adult.

"It would be easy for me to blame my father, but I have learned from my past experiences," I told him. "I know that who I was as a child shaped who I am today. If I'd had a different life growing up, I wouldn't have found myself mentoring. I love my life and what I have done for myself and others."

"I think we are more alike than I thought," Anthony said.

"Very much so. And I'm not done learning either. You have so much to show me yourself. I grow every day by my experience with you," I assured him.

"Me?" he asked.

I have come a long way since I started to mentor others. I have grown in such miraculous ways. I know none of it would have been possible without the people I've mentored pushing me to reach my goals.

"Did you know that when I met Jose, I had not graduated from college?" I asked. "Actually, I had never even completed a college course."

Anthony's jaw slackened. "No, I didn't know that. Do you have a degree now?"

"Yes, I do. I have a few degrees on different levels of studies. But I would never have reached that goal if it had not been for Jose."

At the time, I was helping Jose prepare for his college. He had asked me what my degree was in. I didn't have a college degree. In fact, I had very little experience in even taking college courses.

Jose was shocked.

I had spent so much time with Jose, pushing for him to go to school. Yet, I didn't have a degree of my own. When he pushed me about it, I informed him that I had tried but was unable to complete a degree.

I was barely able to make it out of high school. I have attention-deficit/hyperactivity disorder, better known as ADHD. I felt that I wasn't cut out for college.

Jose did not accept that answer from me.

I had to let Jose know that I was already in my thirties, and I already had a career. Even if I wanted to go, it was too late for me. I wouldn't be a successful candidate for college, especially with my ADHD.

Jose told me that it was an excuse.

It's sometimes hard to hear the criticism that others have of you. As much as you want to push the criticism away, you have to be open to it. I knew it. It was an excuse. I knew he was right.

I've never had anyone question me about college. After high school, I looked into my options to become a police officer. When I completed my training, I joined the police force. The thought of college had become a thought of the past.

Jose explained to me that I had made a difference in so many people's lives for the better. I used my ADHD as a crutch just like Jose had hidden behind his parents' deaths and not having legal status as a way to settle in life. I felt in my heart that a career at Jack in the Box wasn't the answer for Jose. Now Jose believed that a life without a college degree wasn't the answer for me. Together, we wouldn't settle.

It occurred to me then that Jose was challenging me, just like I challenged everyone else. Being a mentor works both ways. As our journey progressed, I knew I was going to make Jose a better person. Now I believed as our journey continued, Jose would make me a better person as well.

"And that's when you went to college?" Anthony asked.

"Yes. I actually enrolled at the same time as Jose. I started college when he started college, and we did homework together every weekend."

"What did you end up graduating with?"

"I earned my bachelor's degree in business management with an emphasis on organizational behavior, but I didn't stop there. Because Jose had encouraged me to go back to college, I wanted to reach my highest potential. I tried taking the LSAT because I wanted to go to law school. My test score wasn't high enough, and I was not accepted. I was discouraged, and Jose encouraged me to press on. So I kept going. I went on to earn a master's degree in public administration and a then a doctorate of education in leadership."

"Was it worth it to go back to college later than most people?" Anthony asked.

"It opened up the possibilities of jobs and people I met. I changed more than ever, as my eyes were opened to how to be a better leader. It was all because of Jose. Anthony, I want you to know that when we look at each other, we should see ourselves as equals. We shouldn't compare each other based on how much money we make, how many friends we have, or what house we live in.

"We see each other based on who we are as people and where we want to go. As friends and mentors, we constantly strive to help everyone meet their goals.

"Jose was a man who many felt was on a dead-end road. I saw him as a man who could achieve greatness. He now works as a deputy public defender for the county of San Diego. He's married and has a child, with another one on the way.

"We are where we are now not because of ourselves but because of each other. You can have that same impact on me that Jose did."

Anthony's mood had completely changed. I knew these stories were sometimes hard to believe, but they were all true. I wouldn't inspire Anthony with false hopes.

Chapter Four

Mentoring Doesn't Stop With You

I had spoken to Anthony on the phone, and he stated he had something to talk to me about. I didn't press him for details, because his voice didn't sound urgent. I had some exciting news to tell him myself.

As he walked in the door, I was excited to see him again. Our meeting times and places had become routine. We felt comfortable with each other, and our conversations tended to become more personal. Talking about the weather, news programs, world events, and good new restaurants were not uncommon for us.

"What's up, Anthony?" I asked.

"Not much," he casually said.

"School going all right?"

"Yeah, it's tough, but I'm working at it every day."

He looked tired, but in the good way. He was working hard, both at his job and at school. I saw the progress in him, and I always made sure he knew how I felt.

"That is great to hear. I'm proud of you," I assured him.

"You always say that," he said with a smirk.

"I always mean it! I'm also interested to know what you'd like to talk to me about."

Anthony's smirk disappeared from his face, which let me know he was about to say something serious.

"It's about a guy I met growing up," Anthony began. "His name is Manny. I've talked to him from time to time. I can see he is trying to get on the right path, but he is fighting some demons. I was hoping you could mentor him."

Anthony was confronting me on what to do. Even though I respected his decision to reach out to me, I knew Anthony was fully capable of mentoring someone on his own.

"Why don't you mentor him?" I asked.

Anthony's eyes dilated. "I don't know if I could ever do that."

"Of course you could," I said. "Why not?"

"Because I'm not experienced like you are," he responded.

"Anthony, you have all the experience you need. Remember, you are a developing leader. It is important for you to be a curious learner throughout your journey. You said you see yourself in Manny?"

"Yeah, he reminds me of a lot of the struggles I have gone through."

"And you have found your way, right?" I pointed out.

"Yeah, but it was with your help."

"Exactly. Now Manny can find his way with *your* help. You are an upcoming leader. Do your best to model the ideal behavior and connect with those you can encourage and develop."

"You think I can do that?" he questioned.

"Yes, Anthony," I answered. "Take Manny under your wing. Involve him in projects and the environment of your life so he can learn and grow as a leader as well. I have seen it done so many times before. You remember Jose? He mentored someone too. His name was Agustin. Agustin would go on to do great things and have an enormous influence over my life. To this day, I have never seen someone endure such a painful event yet serve others so passionately."

I then told Anthony the story of my experiences with Agustin. I met

Agustin back in the early 2000s when he was scammed at a local trade school. He was pressured into attending the overpriced trade school because he was told he could earn a bachelor's degree. He signed up and started attending classes. However, he quickly saw that it was not so good. The program would be more expensive and time consuming than he was originally told. Worse off, it wasn't a bachelor's degree program. The trade school was only equipped to award certifications for a specific field of study.

He only attended classes for one week before he withdrew from his classes. The trade school continued to bill him as if he were still attending. I ended up getting involved to advocate for him. A friend of Agustin's had told me about the story, and I was more than willing to become involved. We used the local news to assist us and expose this story. It worked, because Agustin ended up having his money refunded. Agustin would later enroll in San Diego City College.

Agustin had grown up in a rough neighborhood without the influence of a father. His dad walked out on the family when Agustin was only three years old. He therefore had no one to teach him about life and the difference between right and wrong. Throughout his life, he had very minimal contact with his father. Those interactions stopped in his adult life when he saw how poorly his father treated his mother.

Despite his upbringing, Agustin was trying to make a better life for himself. He had struggled to graduate high school, as he was making ends meet by working at a Jack in the Box. (Not the same location as Jose; this detail is purely coincidental.) Agustin lacked the influence of a father growing up.

Although he was around the gang and drug scene, he had worked hard to distance himself from that life, as many people he knew were in prison. It was obvious to me that the best way to mentor Agustin would be through the help of Jose. Jose was now in his last year at San Diego City College and was working on his application for San Diego State University. Jose had a clear goal of becoming a lawyer, and his future was bright.

I knew Jose would be good for Agustin, because Agustin had talked about becoming a paralegal one day. Jose also had the same negative influences that Agustin did, and Jose could share his story of how he had overcome those obstacles. After their first meeting, my initial instincts were right, as Jose and Agustin had a lot in common. They connected on their interest in the law and even knew a lot of the same people. They clicked right away.

Agustin decided to follow in Jose's footsteps and enroll in San Diego City College, with his ultimate goal of becoming an attorney. Jose let Agustin know that he would be there for him every step of the way. Agustin succeeded and graduated from San Diego City College.

He was then accepted into San Diego State University and started his degree in psychology. During that time, Agustin also began working as a teaching assistant at the San Diego Juvenile Detention Facility to pay for his living expenses and college tuition.

In August 2007, Agustin was in his early twenties and going into his last year of SDSU when tragedy struck. Agustin's fourteen-year-old brother, Javier, was shot and killed in their neighborhood through a random act of violence. One Sunday night before he passed, Agustin's mother called to say she had found Javier next to a nearby streetlight. After arriving at the hospital shortly after midnight, Agustin got the news that his brother hadn't made it.

When Agustin's little brother was killed, right away Agustin and I knew very well what God would ask of us. We were to lead Javier's friends. The strongest love we could ever demonstrate to Javier would be the commitment to his friends. We would commit ourselves to be there for his friends as we had hoped to be there for Javier himself.

During the funeral service, it became evident that God would bond us closely with Javier's best friends. God used the grieving process to knit our hearts together with theirs.

For the week during his funeral and burial, Agustin and I would be together almost nonstop. Most of the time words were never spoken, just tears. We wept with Javier's friends over the loss of Javier.

Javier was buried on Thursday, and on that following Saturday, Agustin and I met with his friends. There were about fifteen of them present. We created a notebook for each of them, which contained a picture of Javier. The words, "In Loving Memory of Javier Quiroz," appeared on the cover. The first page of the notebook was a letter written to Javier. Friends were encouraged to write to him. They could speak out things they wanted to tell him, goals they had for themselves, or regrets about their time together.

People took turns reading out loud what they had written in the book. It was amazing to see how much love Javier had on Earth. It seemed everyone had also made a vow that he would go to school and make his family proud. Prior to Javier's death, these same people would have never made these promises. Many of them had previously spoken about the desire to drop out of school. Now, they were rallying behind each other and promising to help everyone stick to their new goals.

The next page of each notebook had the following verses:

> The Lord replied, "If you return to me, I will restore you so you can continue to serve me. If you speak words that are worthy, you will be my spokesman. You are to influence them; do not let them influence you! They will fight against you like an attacking army, but I will make you as secure as a fortified wall. They will not conquer you, for I will protect and deliver you. I, the Lord, have spoken! Yes, I will certainly keep you safe from these wicked men. I will rescue you from their cruel hands." (Jeremiah 15:19–21 New King James Version)

> Where there is ignorance of God, crime runs wild; but what a wonderful thing it is for a nation to know and keep his laws. (Proverbs 29:18 NKJV)

The Lord is for me, so I will not be afraid. What can mere mortals do to me? Yes, the Lord is for me; he will help me. I will look in triumph at those who hate me. It is better to trust the Lord than to put confidence in people. (Psalm 118:6–8 NKJV)

The eyes of the Lord search the whole earth in order to strengthen those whose hearts are fully committed to him. What a fool you have been! From now on, you will be at war." (2 Chronicles 16:9 NKJV)

So let us go out to him outside the camp and bear the disgrace he bore. For this world is not our home; we are looking forward to our city in heaven, which is yet to come. (Hebrews 13:13–14 NKJV)

Behold, the whirlwind of the Lord Goes forth with fury, a continuing whirlwind; It will fall violently on the head of the wicked. The fierce anger of the Lord will not return until He has done it. And until He has performed the intents of His heart. In the latter days you will consider it. (Jeremiah 30:23–24 NKJV)

And he will turn the hearts of the fathers to the children, and the hearts of the children to their fathers, lest I come and strike the earth with a curse." (Malachi 4:6 NKJV)

Agustin could have given up then. He could have accepted the fact that his brother was gone and turned to a darker path. Instead, Agustin poured himself tirelessly into the community. He launched an antiviolence campaign called PowerMentor Mobile Outreach. He was spreading the message of change and responsibility with words and encouragement, not violence.

He spoke openly about his thoughts on life. He said we should never live our days like tomorrow is promised to us. Agustin thought this was a selfish way of thinking—for the right reasons. When you put your life first, you are able to therefore give back to someone in a positive way. He had no one to turn to when things got tough.

Agustin was also able to use the memories of his childhood in his mentoring as well. It served as motivation for him to help others who had the same struggles. He would be that person who wouldn't be too busy to throw a baseball around, watch a movie, or talk on the phone. Holidays and birthdays wouldn't have to go by unnoticed.

His work did not go unnoticed as his leadership became more prevalent in the community. Eventually, Javier's killer was brought to justice, and charges were filed. The killer said that he thought Javier was somebody else. Agustin would never be able to use this explanation for any type of closure.

Agustin would attend the court hearings later while he was in law school. Ultimately, he was learning about the law in the classroom while watching it play out in the courtroom for the murder of his little brother. He had to relive the pain when hearing the testimonies of the killers. It only inspired him more to find justice in the lives of other families that had been affected like his.

Agustin continued to pursue his dream. He attended California Western School of Law and received his law degree. He is now a deputy district attorney for the county of San Diego.

"Anthony, you remember Jose's story?" I asked. "Could you believe in the beginning that Jose could be such an inspiration for one person?"

"I believe it now," he said.

"And when you come such a long way, you will always have a group of supporters to help you through anything."

"So I could really have this effect on someone?"

"Of course you could. And the story doesn't stop there. Just like Jose would influence Agustin, Agustin would influence a man named Irving Pedroza."

I then told Anthony the story of Irving. During the fall of 2010, during Agustin's second year of law school, he would have the opportunity to become acquainted with Irving Pedroza who had just entered law school. They met at a La Raza Student Association event; Agustin served as the president of the organization. La Raza was great for students because it was a Latino Student Association within the law school. It brought people together who had similar backgrounds, and they did community service work.

Irving immediately approached Agustin because he felt something inside that they had some kind of connection. Agustin told Irving that if he ever needed anything to let him know.

Agustin would reflect that his immediate impression of Irving was that he was a humble and sincere person.

Irving recalled that he continued to encounter Agustin. Irving remarked that Agustin was always interested in how he was doing. During one such conversation, Irving began to share some personal family struggles. He noted that Agustin was a particularly good listener. After Irving shared with Agustin, he felt a sense that everything would be okay, and it created an immediate bond in their new friendship. Because previously, Irving was not able to open up to others, he now found this therapeutic. Law school was an entirely different and new world for him, and making himself vulnerable by sharing personal struggles was uncharted territory.

At the time, Irving did not think peers in law school would be able to relate to his circumstances, but what he didn't know was that he would have much more in common with Agustin that he thought.

Irving was very similar to Agustin. He graduated from high school but grew up in a rough neighborhood in Escondido. He experienced domestic violence in the home from his mom and dad. Also, his older brother was diagnosed with schizophrenia. On one occasion, his brother tried to choke Irving to death when he was only a teen. He also struck Irving multiple times, landing him in the hospital.

Like Agustin as well, Irving was the first in his family to attend college.

At the time, Irving did not think peers in law school would be able to relate to his circumstances. He was a law student who was a Latino from the inner city.

"To this day," I said to Anthony, "Agustin has been a great influence on Irving. He helped him find purpose in his life. Irving finished law school, passed the bar, and now practices immigration law."

Anthony seemed inspired. "I think I could be that person for Manny."

"I know you could. You see, Anthony, mentoring doesn't stop with you and me. You have found this process yourself and can now go into the world and help others. It also brings a sense of accountability for yourself, because Manny will hold you accountable if you do not practice what you teach him."

I also needed to let Anthony know that I wouldn't just disappear. If Manny accepted Anthony's offer to find the right path, he would join a fraternity of brothers.

"Anthony, if you decide to take this on, I will be there for you every step of the way. We all work together at PowerMentor, helping each other problem solve and strategize in mentoring others."

Anthony received what I said with a sigh of relief; he would not have to go it alone in mentoring Manny.

Anthony changed the subject, as a lightbulb seemed to go off.

"Speaking of that, you said you had something to say to me?" he asked.

In fact, I had some exciting news for Anthony. "Anthony, I have seen many signs that you have changed your life. Your studies at the community college are going well, and you've shown interest in continuing your studies at a four-year university. I'm excited to let you know that I have completed your paperwork to get you a court appearance before a judge."

I believed that Anthony had already changed so much of his life. I told Anthony I would get his felony removed, and I had stuck to that. I had gathered all the information necessary and filled out the paperwork.

Anthony's eyes lit up. "Are you serious?" he asked. It was all he was able to get out. He had completely jumped out of his chair.

"Yes, I am!" I told him.

When he was finally able to sit back down, it seemed like he had a list of questions. "So when is it? Is my felony going to disappear? What should I wear?"

"Anthony, Anthony, slow down," I said. "We are only beginning the process to have your felony reduced to a misdemeanor. Then, eventually, we can consider having a pardon so there is not record whatsoever."

"I have changed so much."

"I know. You see now, Anthony, even your small accomplishments are big accomplishments in your journey. Keep up the good work; it's leading you to where you want to go."

"I will keep this motivation as I go forward."

CHAPTER FIVE

Mentees Learning to Mentor Others

I wanted to take the time to teach Anthony about the steps of mentoring. He was already into the process, and he didn't even know it.

"Anthony, mentoring someone is a great responsibility," I told him.

"And you think I'm ready?" he asked.

"Of course I do, because you've already passed the first stage of mentoring."

"How?"

"You found something that you felt drawn to. There was something about Manny that made you remember him and bring him to our attention. So now it's up to you to establish a mentoring relationship with him."

"He could not want to accept the process," he said.

Anthony brought up a great point. There had been many people along the years who I knew were ready but were resistant. I have fought very hard for people and did not give up easily.

"You have to believe in what you do," I said to him. "You are doing it for a very good reason. I know I have never given up on people. Even years after talking to people, they know they can still see me as a friend. This reminds me of another Jose, not Jose Orozco, but Jose Antonio, a fifteen-year-old I met in the early 1990s."

I had met Jose Antonio through the Bridge the Gap Boxing program in El Cajon, a program I had started while serving as a police officer. We had bonded instantly. He would open up to me about his rough upbringing and the poor living conditions he had experienced in Tijuana. After our time together, Jose Antonio was forced to go back to Mexico due to his illegal status in the United States. I had vowed to stay in touch with Jose Antonio, but we drifted apart.

Over the years, I had tried to get in touch with Jose Antonio to see how he was doing. I had been to Tijuana many times. While there, I would try to contact him, but nothing seemed to work. Jose Antonio was dealing with his family struggles in Tijuana.

His mother was in and out of institutions for her mental health problems. His brothers were young enough that they were able to be cared for in an orphanage. Hopefully, they would have a chance at a better life. Because Jose Antonio was too old for the orphanage, he had to find his own means to survive. Unfortunately, it meant turning to life on the streets in Tijuana.

On one of my trips in 2003, I encountered a man who appeared homeless and drug addicted. He was washing windows on the street for money. It was Jose Antonio. I gave him my number and promised him I would help him. All he had to do was make the call.

He never did.

In 2006, I was back in Tijuana filming a documentary on the correlation between corruption and poverty. At the time, I was teaching a college criminal justice ethics class. I took the students from my class with me so they could experience interviewing members of a very poverty-stricken area and document it on film. My friends on the trip knew about my story with Jose Antonio. It had been just over ten years since my first encounter with him. I had prayed we would be reunited again.

Sure enough, I saw a homeless man on the street. He appeared to be Jose Antonio, but so much time had passed. I rolled down the window and called out his name. He immediately looked at me, called out my name, and started running toward me.

I jumped out of the car and gave Jose Antonio the strongest embrace I have ever experienced. His skin was worn from the sun. His clothes were dirty from his life on streets. His hair and body reeked. For me, it didn't matter. None of this entered my mind when hugging him. All I cared about was getting Jose Antonio the care he needed.

When he took a seat in the car, I saw tears streaming down his face. I knew then that his prayers had been answered as well as mine. We were going to get Jose Antonio back on the right path

"Did Jose Antonio stop living on the streets?" Anthony asked after I told the story.

"Yes, he did. But for him, the hardships did not stop there. I'm sharing this story with you now because I want you to know that it might be hard. You have yet to learn about Manny's story. You may have known him casually when you were younger, but you may not be privy to what he has endured in his life. No matter how bad it gets, we can't give up. Jose Antonio had to tell our team about his life on the streets. Some of his stories were very hard to hear. He spoke to us about drug use, prostitution, and robbery. It was enough for anyone to turn away, but we didn't. In fact, the one person who drew even closer to Jose Antonio was Agustin!"

"But he changed?" Anthony asked.

"He did, but remember that you can't change the past. You can only help Manny change his future. Jose Antonio had to live with the choices he made. After we placed him in a drug rehabilitation program for years of Heroin use, he tested positive for both hepatitis C and HIV. From accepting the mentoring process, he was able to come to terms with his choices and make better decisions about his future. He was able to know what unconditional love and friendship meant. He completed rehabilitation but still had a long journey ahead."

"And it took ten years?"

"Yes. Until I felt that Jose Antonio was on the right path, it took a good ten years," I told him. "You know the second step of mentoring is planting the seeds. Some people don't understand why someone would want to mentor them. I think you felt this way. Didn't you, Anthony?"

"Yes, I did. I felt like you were someone very successful. You didn't need someone like me in your life. I had done a lot of things in my past that I wasn't proud of. I felt a lot of times that I wasn't worthy enough to be your friend."

"I'm sure you can understand where Jose Antonio was coming from. Your role as a mentor will be to encourage that person to do better with the life he has. This isn't about who has done more, seen more, or accomplished more. Mentoring is about where you can take your life. We can do that by walking alongside each other—as equals."

"Are you ever nervous that people will let you down?" he asked.

"It's a fair question. I have the highest hopes for everyone I mentor. I want them to succeed and thrive. I get satisfaction in knowing that they have come such a long way.

"When I know my mentee didn't quite reach where I know they can, it's discouraging. I can't say it's necessarily disappointing, because I always have hope he can still make it. The toughest stage of your process as a mentor is going to be sitting and watching. You can't do everything for him. You have to trust that he will follow through on the guidance you give him. There is a learning process from such things as trial and error and temptation."

"I feel like I can be a good mentor to Manny, because I have been through a lot in my life. It should be very easy for him to relate to me and be proud of my progress."

"I agree, Anthony. He might feel as though because you've done it, then he can do it too. Sometimes a mentor can have trouble listening to what his mentee has done in his life. It's easy for one to have a reaction that can hurt the other person. Manny could very well see himself in you, and therefore, he can receive inspiration for moving on. He won't feel as ashamed of his life when he knows he has you around."

"Now that I have all the steps laid out for me, what would be one thing that you would recommend?" Anthony asked.

This was hard for me to answer, because I have met so many people over the years. Everyone is different, but still, you want the same thing for them. You also know that each mentor needs to follow his own path.

"I would say, never give up on anyone. I cannot tell you how many times people have told me I was such a good friend and mentor to them because I was always there for them."

"Do you ever feel like you're too busy? You had school and family and friends and mentoring," he said.

"Anthony, it's a great adventure! The friends you make and the experiences you have with people will never seem like a burden. Only you will know how to handle your own schedule and what you can bring people.

"Mentoring can be painful as you see your mentee endure the consequences of his decisions or the struggles of day-to-day life. Anthony, remember Jose Antonio who you have worked with during many projects in Mexico?"

"Yes, I remember him well. I really like him."

"I remember seeing how well the both of you worked together. With Jose Antonio, there were ups and downs. Jose Antonio accompanied us on many humanitarian projects throughout Mexico, and he always impacted people he would meet. Everyone loved him and was shocked when he shared his story of living on the streets. Jose Antonio bounced back living drug free, and most would see him as a person who had never lived on the street. He looked healthy, strong, energetic, and so much fun to be around. He and I grew very close, and I considered him like a brother. Remember a few weeks ago when Jose Antonio joined us for some outreach projects in Tijuana?"

"Yes, of course I remember."

"During our last project, I could see his health was deteriorating from the hepatitis C and HIV. He was fatigue, and shared with me that he felt he was not getting better. I tried to be optimistic with him, as he was still young in his thirties, and we had hoped he had many more years. During that outreach, Jose Antonio gave it his all, high energy so that he could be a blessing to the young people he was encouraging. Remember how he was shadow boxing with some of the young people he was mentoring?"

"Yes, he seemed full of energy!"

"Anthony, yesterday, to my shock, I received a phone call from Jose Antonio's brothers tell me that Jose Antonio had passed away. I was stunned, and myself, along with Pastor Jose Villaescuza, just cried. We were so saddened because we had been through so much with him."

"I am shocked," Anthony said. "I can't believe he is gone. I remember how close he and Pastor Jose were."

Pastor Jose Villaescuza and I had met years ago when gang members had gunned down a fifteen-year-old boy named Moises from his church youth group. After receiving calls from community members asking that we assist Moises's family, I went to the neighborhood to find the family and offer support. While canvasing the area, I happened upon Pastor Jose, who was grieving the loss of Moises and assisting the family.

Our connecting was immediate, and our friendship was locked in for life. Pastor Jose and I were likeminded and immediately coordinated our efforts in antiviolence projects, movie nights in the park, and so many more outreach projects. Pastor Jose is such an amazing person, and his wife and kids are just as amazing. Because of their strong family, Jose Antonio always admired that and felt a part of that.

"Anthony, this will be a challenging time for us. Pastor Jose and I will attend his funeral in Tijuana and have the opportunity to share all of the great things about Jose Antonio's life and all of the people he impacted during his life. We will be honored to share the greatness of Jose Antonio and offer support to his family."

"I am so sorry, Kevin," Anthony said. "I cannot imagine how you feel. I too will miss Jose Antonio so much."

"He is in a better place, but it is still hard. We have to keep perspective and never forget how he lived his life after most people would have given up, Jose Antonio always fought to grow and serve others."

CHAPTER SIX
Letting Go

I had another meeting with Anthony. I was counting on him to bring me some crucial information so we could move forward with his court proceedings.

When I saw him coming, I noticed that he was empty-handed.

"Anthony, how are you doing?" I asked.

"Pretty good," he responded. "How are you?"

"I'm doing well. It's nice to see you again, even though you seem empty-handed. Do you have that paperwork for me?"

"No, I don't." Anthony shrugged.

"Anthony, I was really counting on that paperwork today."

"I know. I've just been doing a lot of things, and I need a break. I've kind of been procrastinating."

"Anthony, procrastination is our greatest barrier, and you must stop it dead in its tracks, or it will completely immobilize you!" I told him.

"For me, procrastination is just something I do so I can relax a little," he explained.

"Procrastination is more than that, Anthony. It's the putting off of a task that *needs* to be done. The greatest challenge for those who are procrastinators is their rationale that a task can wait. We all know what happens: it never gets done, or it doesn't get done on time. Are you ready for that history test you were telling me about?"

"I'm going to do the rest of my studying tonight. I haven't had time."

"Anthony, you have to see that procrastinating can affect your entire life. It is not simply putting a thing off that is the destroyer. It is the inability to prioritize and plan your day productively so that you can accomplish everything intended."

"So what happens when I need to do homework, but I want to play video games?" he asked.

"Well, Anthony, the opposite of procrastination is productivity. So if we focus on what is right instead of what is wrong, then we must focus on productivity instead of focusing on the problem of procrastination. We are drawn to that which we focus on. If we focus on procrastination, we will gravitate toward that and will not be able to overcome this shortcoming."

"Sometimes doing something else helps me stay focused. You said you had ADHD. You had to have moments where you procrastinated and strayed away from your schoolwork."

"Yes, Anthony. You have a good point," I admitted. "I always had to focus on being productive and build a foundation that was not compatible with that of a procrastinator. The real issue was to ask myself what was important to me and what things I could do to offer the greatest return on my investment to the time spent.

"For example, my goal was to finish college. So I had to be productive in my homework, networking, and personal and professional development. Now, if my goal were to move up in my organization, then I would need to focus my time on that goal. If my goal were to build a strong family, then I must be productive in the home."

"But you're an adult. It's easier for you now."

"When I was younger, your age, I was the same way. I was known for starting projects and never finishing them. I am now known for finishing everything I set my mind to, and that took discipline. What I had to do was reinvent myself. When I reflected on what was the root cause, I could identify that my mind was running a million miles an hour, and as I would have something pop in my mind, I would have every intention of planning a project and completing it. However, as soon as one idea came into fruition, another was right there in line."

"I'm the same way. How did you change?"

"I always stopped and asked myself, 'What do I want to be known for in my life? Do I want to accomplish great things or be known as a person who was all talk and no action?' I chose to be known for accomplishing my goals and doing anything I set my mind to!"

"Be a doer," Anthony said.

"Yes! That is what I'm asking you to do. Be determined to be a doer, not a talker. This will require you to begin to develop the skills that will completely remove any opportunity for you to become a procrastinator. When you get in the game, you will be so engaged that you will not even think about not doing what needs to be done."

"I just need to get away from the video games."

"And Facebook?" I prodded.

"Yeah, of course," he agreed. "Did you use Facebook?"

"Yeah, of course. Probably the number-one time waster is playing video games and being consumed with social media networks such as Facebook. In moderation, Facebook can yield returns if it is used effectively. However, if I am spending time on Facebook and avoiding accomplishing tasks that yield greater return, then I am not prioritizing effectively. Video games are by far the greatest dilemma of our time. It can become an addiction. Consider some of the games that stimulate our minds and reconsider the fact that one could be in the game of life and play for real instead of pretend. Imagine the possibilities."

"I would get a lot of things done if I didn't play video games," Anthony joked. "I could probably get all the chores done around the house that my mom has been begging me to get to."

"Well, Anthony, another thing you can work on is making what's important around you, important to you. What I mean by this is if you tell people that you will do something for them, then do it. Do not be all talk and no action. Let your words match your actions."

"Okay, I should have written this all down," he noted.

I took out some paper and a pen from my briefcase and handed them to Anthony. "Well, why don't we do this? I'll ask you some questions about getting organized and establishing priorities. After you write it down, tell me your response," I suggested.

"Okay," he agreed.

"Every day, make a list using your smartphone, pen and paper, or whatever means you are comfortable with. Each day, you should have daily tasks, and each week have your larger priorities. This is the first question. After prioritizing your list with three things in mind, which is most important? Which can be accomplished quickly? Which is required in order for other to be accomplished?"

After taking a couple seconds, Anthony gave me his answer. "Three things that are important to me are working, going to school, and helping with my family. The most important is school, because it's going to help me get a better job and provide for my family. Helping with my family is the quickest, because I can do things around the house like the dishes or mowing the lawn."

"What is a good way to extend your personal productivity?"

"Limit my time on Facebook and playing video games. I'll pay attention to how much time they take up, and I'll make sure any time I spend on there is a wise investment. I'll stop putting things off as much."

"How does procrastination prevent you from being a good mentor?" I asked.

"I think that the best part of being a role model is being productive, connecting with people that are productive, and involving myself and others into worthwhile projects," he said.

"That's very effective. Attacking procrastination, that nasty habit, can cost you a lot of time, energy, and frustration! Putting things off seldom improves the quality of your work. In fact, knowing you have something to do that should already have been done just increases stress."

"Kevin, as long as you help me, I will always know what to do," he said.

"Anthony the decisions are yours to make. I can only help you along the way," I told him. "There were many times that I wanted to tell Jose Orozco what decisions he should make. Even now, there are things I hear and see, and I say, 'No, Jose, do it this way.' I have to keep coming back to the fact that Jose is in charge of his own life. It is his life, not mine. Just like this is your life. I can teach you right from wrong, but it's you who has to choose right from wrong."

"How can you do that?" Anthony asked.

"For me, I have to entrust Jose to God. I have strong faith in God and believe He has Jose in His grip. Now, if I genuinely believe that, I have to let go. Letting go is perhaps the hardest part of mentorship. We want to protect the mentored, making sure all of their decisions are the best. We undermine their ability to grow by not allowing them to make their own mistakes."

"Do you have to let me go?" Anthony asked.

"As hard as it is, we have to let go. For me, I have to let God take charge. I have to pray for Jose daily and just be there if he ever needs a pillar to lean on. When you have found your path, I will do the same for you."

— — —

The context of the work of PowerMentor in communities can be evidenced by a speech I gave at a City Heights antiviolence event after a number of young teens had been killed over a one-year period in East San Diego. Here is an excerpt of that speech:

> Why are more and more young people engaging in such crimes of violence? When we talk with young people who have perpetrated random acts of violence against their peers, we notice a common thread. They lack a positive role model, they don't have purpose, and they don't see a future for their lives. We believe that greater love has no parent than to believe in their child more than their child believes in himself. Whether you're a parent, an uncle, aunt, brother, sister, schoolteacher, or mentor, you have the ability to believe in someone more than he believes in himself.
>
> As you hear from families today who have had their children snatched from them, think about the person who is capable of taking that life. Think about what he lacked that caused him to make such a decision to violently kill another without even considering any consequence. We have seen many young people who were on the path to a destructive life. They were destined for prison, held no hope, found no encouragement, and could see no future. And yet, many of these same young people found someone who believed in them, found someone who dared to walk alongside of them, and found someone who had the courage to rise up and mentor them.

Many of these young people were caught up in gangs, filled with hatred, and yet the power of a mentor believing in them conquered the fear that caused them to become so callous and so destructive. For San Diego inner-city neighborhoods, many of these young people who dared to change the direction of their lives, dared not only to dream dreams but find the courage to make them happen, and they're with us here today. From high-school dropout to law student, from prison to college graduate, from gang member to schoolteacher, and the list goes on and on.

To all of the parents who are here today, we ask you to consider that if you are not capturing the hearts of your children, the streets will capture their hearts for you. For uncles and aunts, brothers and sisters, if you do not capture the hearts of your nieces, your nephews, your brothers and sisters, the streets will capture their hearts, and we will all have failed them. The consequences will be found in neighborhood violence, as we've seen. For young people who are here today who cannot see a positive future for themselves, we ask you to find a positive role model who believes in you more than you believe in yourselves.

To everyone who is here today, it's time that we begin to see the greatness in each other instead of constantly seeking out each other's flaws. We must see the greatness of our communities instead of holding on to things that divide us. Now more than ever, families are facing some of the toughest times ever. We must take responsibility for our communities; we must have a change of heart and a change in our mind-set. If you know a young person who's heading down the wrong path and you're not able to reach him, you don't know how, call someone who does know how to help. By helping him, you give him hope, and you spare him from a lifestyle of violence.

For those who have committed crimes against young people like Javier Quiroz, Darnell Smith, Moises Lopez, Monique Palmer, Michael Taylor, and others, they must be held accountable for their actions. For anyone who knows who killed any of these young people, your silence is the very thing destroying our neighborhoods. No one has been brought to justice in most of these cases that you hear about today because of silence. The greatest thing we can do for these families represented here, along with our communities, is to hope and pray that a courageous person who knows what happened will rise up and go to the police so that the police can help.

After sharing this speech with Anthony, I told him, "You too must make a decision to change your life and rise up from the circumstance you have found yourself growing up in. I am committed to believing in you more than you believe in yourself!"

"Kevin, that speech was so moving because it has such profound meaning to me. Some of the people you mentioned in your speech, I knew them, like Javier. I remember when he was killed. Something has to change, Kevin, and I am seeing so much."

"Anthony, letting go of the past and looking forward to the future begins with hope. But remember that hope is not a strategy. You will have to see things very differently. That is why I have exposed you to so many different things over the past two years to stimulate your mind. For example, remember the river rafting trip in Costa Rica?"

"Of course, how could I forget that? … I grew so much from that trip and had never experienced anything like that. It is like when we first got in the raft, I did not want to let go of the shore because it was scary seeing the rapids. But after we took off, the way we all worked together to steer the raft … we seemed to all work in sync."

"Yes, Anthony, each of us was doing our part, and then we all get to where we want to go in life. Remember some of the rapids and how much they tossed our raft so powerfully. Yet, by doing what we were trained to do, we never flipped; we just kept riding the rough rapids over and over again. After a while, it was like nothing; the more we conquered, the more confident we became.

"Recently, I participated in a leadership retreat, and one of the activities included sharing some truths with the others. When it was my turn, I revealed my fear of water that I have had all of my life after a few experiences as a child. The first experience occurred when I was about eight years old. My dad was a firefighter, and our family attended the firefighters' convention each year. During this occasion, some of the firefighters began playing catch with me at a swimming pool. I slipped through the arms of the firefighter who was to catch me and landed in the water after hitting my head on the side of the pool.

"A second incident occurred when my mom placed my siblings and me in swimming lessons. I was very small for my age and could not touch the bottom of the pool. I would hold on to the edges of the pool to stay afloat. To try and force me to learn to swim, the instructors would step on my fingers to keep me from grabbing the edges. I was deathly afraid. During one event, all of the parents came to see how we had progressed. We were to jump off of the high dive. Some children did not want to climb the high dive, and they were not forced. For some reason, I felt compelled to do it. I climbed the ladder, and while on the diving board, I was shaking. My mom could see the fear written all over me. I looked down, and I can still remember the lifeguard's name—Julie.

She motioned for me to jump, and when I finally mustered up enough courage, I jumped, but I slipped through her hands. Because I could not tread water, I went under. She tried grabbing for me, and I clung to her by grabbing a handful of hair. She wrestled to gain control of me and helped me to the side of the pool. My mom praised me for me effort in jumping. I was so scared.

"As time went by, all of my siblings had learned to swim, and in the summer, we would go to the public pool. During one such swim, I would float on a ball so I could tread water. Someone dove in and unintentionally kicked the ball I was holding on to, and down I went again. I just never seemed to take to the water.

"Years ago, friends asked me to go river rafting, and quite frankly, I was too embarrassed to tell them how afraid I was of the water. I went with them and actually liked it. The only problem was that I was terrified of falling out and drowning. As the years passed, I would make it clear to anyone who ever tried to dunk me in the water that I did not like that, and if they did that, the fight would be on.

"Years later, after graduating the police academy, we had a celebration party, and there happened to be a swimming pool right in the center of the gathering. As guys were having fun celebrating, someone came up with the bright idea to throw me in the pool. I was surprised by two good-sized fellow officers grabbing me and others trying to join in. I began kicking and fighting to free myself from their grip. They were saying, 'Throw him in the deep end.' As I heard that, I began fighting harder and struck one friend pretty hard, enough for them to see that I was not happy about this method of fun for them. They let me down, and I explained that I had a major fear of drowning.

"I was awarded the Police Star Award in 1993 for lifesaving when two kids were being swept away by rapid waters in the drainage system. Officers tried rescuing them as we all raced farther downstream, fearing the point that the current would take them under the streets and into the sewage system where they would probably drown due to not being able to breathe. I was dispatched to take a position in the event others missed an opportunity to scoop them out of the water. I prayed, 'God, please don't let them come my way. Help the other officers rescue them.' I then heard on the radio, '206, they are coming your way.' My heart sunk, as I would have to do what I could to save them. I had already taken my police belt off and locked it in my trunk. I had jumper cables and looked for anything I could use to reach out for them to grab. Finally, I was able to have them grab hold of one end of the jumper cables, and I held on to the other end for dear life. A fire truck arrived, throwing me a line, and we pulled them out. A fellow officer commented on my death grip of the concrete drainage ditch. I explained that I was not strong in the water, and I knew I could not help myself if I were to be submerged, let alone rescue others.

"Over the years, I have snorkeled and tried water skiing and continued river rafting to try and face my fear of drowning. When I shared my fear of water during the leadership retreat, others did not believe me because they had viewed photos of my recent river rafting trip. I had just returned from a rafting trip in Costa Rica. I told them to review the pictures more closely, and if they looked closely at my facial expressions, they should be able to see the fear written all over my face … The lesson I have learned is to face my fear head on!"

"That makes sense, Kevin," Anthony noted. "It is like when you had me come along on the outreach trip to El Salvador. That was a crazy trip, and I am not going to lie … that is a scary place. People walking around with machetes and carrying guns and the hardcore gang members everywhere."

"Anthony, if you noticed, we all stayed together as a team, and at times, we had to let go and trust those who were hosting us in their country. It is not easy to let go, and we cannot simply let go without a plan and having the right people and things in place. But in El Salvador, we had loyal people to take care of us while we were there."

"They were great people, Kevin, and I not only learned a lot, but I see how much I grow after every trip we take. Seeing different places around the world is amazing and gives me a different perspective for my life."

"Exactly, Anthony, and that is why I have asked you to be a part of these trips. You are becoming a different person! I see that, and I think you are starting to see things very differently for your life!"

Chapter Seven
Lessons in Leadership

In April 2014, PowerMentor held its annual formal leadership dinner. This dinner is an annual event designed to cause reflecting and help each leader develop and set priorities for the next year. Especially considering the challenges facing Latino males with having the highest high-school dropout rate and the lowest college entrance rate, this is a critical annual meeting.

One-half of Latino males drop out of school before completing their high-school education. In the United States, 41 percent of Latinos ages twenty and older do not have a high-school diploma, compared to 23 percent of their African American peers. Despite the push for minorities to complete their educations, fewer Latino males are enrolling in college than those of other ethnic groups. Latino males tend to be less successful at completing either high school or college than their female Latina counterparts. Students, educators, and parents are equally frustrated by these statistics. When Latinos (as with any other group) drop out before completing high school, they most likely lack the skills and academic background needed for gainful employment.

Young Latino males often do not have a strong support system among their peers or elders to remain in school. In the absence of this support in their communities, an effective support system could include the use of a successful mentoring model. Thinking of success stories of Latino men who understand the importance of education in lifting them out of poverty brings to mind the legendary Cesar Chavez, a renowned Latino activist and advocate of farm workers. When he was ten years old, Cesar's family lost their farm in the Great Depression. They traveled throughout California harvesting fruits and vegetables to keep their family fed.

Teachers and some students called Cesar Chavez "a dumb Chicano," and he soon dropped out of school and joined the US Navy during World War II. After leaving the military, Cesar returned to hard labor working in the fields. He realized that he lacked meaning in his life and knew he needed an education. Cesar began his self-education by studying economics, history, and politics. Later, he established the National Farm Workers Association to fight for the rights of farm workers. Cesar Chavez overcame the obstacles of his youth and led others in the struggle for justice.

Many young Latino males likely find themselves in situations similar to that of Cesar Chavez. However, unlike Cesar, most of them never return to school. Financial constraints and the lack of support systems tend to destroy any dreams they might have of attending college. Other issues are connected to irresponsible decisions in their youth, resulting in unplanned pregnancies, unemployment, and incarceration. Cesar was not the only Latino who had barriers to overcome. Latino men, especially young men, ideally need a strong support system such as one available through successful mentoring.

Gaining definitive insight into the factors associated with the success or failure of the PowerMentor program in preventing young Latino men from dropping out of high school has never been attempted. Latino men who did not participate in the PowerMentor program have never been queried about why they dropped out of high school or the barriers that they perceive as having prevented them from attending college.

Latino men have lower college enrollment rates and academic success and higher college dropout rates than their Caucasian counterparts. The lower college enrollment rates of Latino men point to a problem in the transition from high school to postsecondary education as a significant barrier. Therefore, strategies and models are needed for teachers and parents to use to mentor and assist Latino male students in completing their high-school studies and persuade them to enter college.

With this in mind, our annual dinner was also a time for those who have succeeded in completing college and have now transitioned into their careers to inspire those currently on their journeys.

I first shared the following with the group:

> I hope this is a night that we have some great reflections on all of the accomplishments over the years from each of you. Where we can look at the next five years of our lives as kind of the focus of "what's our plan, what's our journey," for you personally, professionally. We'll have some people speaking and sharing, and each of you is going to get an opportunity to share as well.
>
> Irving is going to share this evening about "Failure Is Not an Option" from an experience that he encountered when he studied as hard as he could after completing law school, took the bar, and unfortunately was unable to pass it the first time. And what that felt like. He is going to share candidly about how much he felt like giving up but what he chose instead to do and what resulted from his efforts.
>
> Agustin will then share his topic: "Mission Accomplished." Sometimes, you go to school, you finish, and then all of a sudden you find yourself in the position and you are met with, "Now what? Am I going to be able to cut this or what?" You have this rude awakening.

Jose will share about his experience when he unexpectedly found himself heading in a different direction as the principal for a charter school. He met great challenges while on this detour; yet, he pressed on and then was diverted again to his original plan of becoming an attorney.

When I look out over this group, I see all of the accomplishments from each of you. Tony, you're in your master's program; Chas, you're in your bachelor's program. Mario, you finished college several years ago and now run your own branch at Chase. You probably never thought you would be in this position now, right? Luis, you are leading your family—your sons, who because of Luis's leadership, one day when they are on their own as they become adults, they will be prone to making the best decisions for their lives. Miguel has his wife and kids; he's got to lead them. He's going to college to be an example for them and working full-time. The list goes on and on.

Some of you come from crazy adversities that you have overcome! Danny, getting ready to get his legal documentation to be in the United States, finally. After how many years of feeling like giving up? Yet, you persevered, and it is now paying off. David, you have been leading your family and working so hard to support them. Now you are nearing receiving your legal documentation as well. Eddie just received his legal status and now is working as a chef. I mean, this room is so filled with such dynamic people, and sometimes I feel like maybe we are not connecting with each other like we could be. We must realize the unbelievable resource that we all have with each other—amazing resources here.

William finished his master's recently. The doors then opened for a promotion with his employer, the City of San Diego. Martin just graduated from San Diego State University. Jose is now attending law school after being mentored by Irving and successfully having his criminal record expunged so that there will no longer be any barriers as he completes law school. Anthony recently filed to have his record expunged, continues to press on to complete San Diego City College and transfer to San Diego State University.

All the different things—we can go on and on and on. Prawit Hess is getting ready to retire as a firefighter. He and his wife want to open a restaurant. Every time you think a door is closing—"Oh, I am retiring"—not so fast, another door is opening.

We can all think about those things. Look at Chit Tway here, who flew in from Utah. All the war trauma he has endured in Burma, and now he's here and working toward finishing up his education, considering either engineering or nursing. Jose M. is serving in the US Marine Corps. Miguel Ramirez here, attending college for graphic design and animation. Ryan works full-time, leading his family and returning to college.

You just look at every single story. Alex is nearing the completion of his bachelor's at Arizona State University. Sometimes I wonder if we recognize the amazing accomplishments. Through my eyes, over the past two decades of watching each of you experience highs and lows, adversity, tears, and making sacrifices. Your progress is remarkable. It's just amazing to see that.

For me, as my life has grown from the profound impact each of you has had on my life, especially in completing my doctorate, finally, which I never thought would happen. So we have a lot to be thankful for, especially each other. Yet, we continue to have a lot of decisions to make individually and collectively. So these next five years are going to be powerful. And again, all of your journeys are different. For some of you, your journey is about your family—leading your family, trying to be for your kids what you wished you would have had when you were young. For some of you, it's your career. Some of you, it's both.

The reality is, we all need to have a purpose, and we want to impact this world. There are so many ways that we can do it through being effective leaders. When you have the opportunity, I would ask you to reflect on the vertical learning we have been talking about. Vertical learning is the transformation of how leaders think, feel, and make sense of the world. It includes the development of both mental complexity and emotional intelligence. We can accelerate this learning by understanding that "how we know" is more important than "what we know," especially when leading through complex change.

Effective leaders of the future must be highly strategic thinkers able to focus on complex problems and opportunities, superb and inspiring communicators with excellent people skills, risk-oriented, and deeply collaborative. This is each of you; that is what we strive to be. Our strategy has been to develop future leaders one person at a time, empowering each of you to be capable of breaking through the glass ceiling, cultivating high-impact innovation, building high-trust relationships, acting with deep courage, and recognizing your ability to transform the organizations that afford you that opportunity. We must reflect and critically think: "How do we navigate through challenging times?"

Mario, how many times have we talked about politics in the workplace? How challenging that is. Miguel, how many times have we talked about it? I mean, it's challenging in the workplace to navigate through that. You know? How do we do that? What's the best way?

I would ask each of you to share a little about where you are in your own journey right now—goals, barriers, whatever you feel comfortable sharing.

Each of the participants would then introduce himself:

"My name is Luis Castillo. I work for Scripps Green Hospital. I have been there for about two years. Like Kevin said, I have a wife and three kids—twelve, six, and five. My focus right now is on them."

"Good afternoon. My name is Anthony Corona. How is everybody doing? I'm in junior college right now. Basically, my goal is to finish junior college, go to San Diego State University, get my bachelor's in political science, and continue to law school. Those are my goals for now."

"My name is Eduardo Del Alto. Right now I am attending school to complete my GED and then go to college. I work at Tender Greens as a sous chef. My goal in five years is to probably become an executive chef, starting my own restaurant. That's my plan."

"Hi, my name is Ryan Gomez. I have a family. I have a three-year-old son, a one-year-old daughter. I work at Sharp HealthCare. My goal for the next five years is to go back to school and get my bachelor's in health care administration."

"Good evening, everyone; my name is Prawit Hess, and I am a firefighter. I met Kevin when I was seventeen years old, so I have known him a long time. I've been fighting fires for probably more than twenty years now. I'm ready to retire. I have a family, and to me, that is very important. Because I can't change the world, but I can change myself. I can change my kids. Last year I was over in Arizona to bury my … I lost nineteen firefighters last year, so I had the opportunity to go back and bury them. But there's a little sticker in the classroom that I saw. I got my phone out and took a picture of it. It says, 'The way the trees grow, the way the limbs are bent, when you bend and tweak the limbs, that's how the trees are going to grow.' And the same is so for your kids. So if you are tough on your kids, it's all right because that's the way they're going to grow up to be. You want them to be honest. You want them to do the right thing. So it really touched my heart when I saw that sticker. My five-year goal is to try to open up a business. For those of you who know me, or don't know me, my wife is half Mexican, and I was born in Thailand. So our kids are half Thai, half Mexican. I want to do something for my kids, and I was inspired by my kids to try to open up a business. So my thought was to open up a restaurant that represents both of them. I want to do something like corn and a side of fried rice. Something like that.

Maybe do a tamale but wrap it with a banana leaf and call it a Thai-male. Something like that. It really inspired me to want to do that.

"As a kid, I was the oldest child, forced in the kitchen. I really hated that. But as an adult, it turns out that I love cooking. And being a firefighter, one of my collateral duties is being on a team. So pretty much, anything that happened around the country that's big—Hurricane Katrina a couple of years ago—I got an opportunity to go to New York. So my job when I go out is pretty much to run the food. So I bring the food to the first responders, because they can't do their jobs if they don't eat. I just fell in love with my job as a firefighter, and yet, I get to do what I love to do, which is food. My five-year plan, that's what I want to do. I want to open up a business, open up a restaurant for my kids. It's going to be Senor Thai.

I interjected, "Prawit came from a very, very rough, rough family life where he was in Thailand and then came over here with his dad, who is American and wasn't very nice to him and his brother at all. Just seeing how much Prawit has overcome adversity has been amazing. And then every time the fires are happening, like recently—every time, I am always thinking, *I can't imagine where Prawit is.* The ability that he has to just hike up trails and fight fires in the heat … unbelievable. But if you ever get the chance to get to know Prawit more, he is a really amazing, amazing individual."

"Hello, everyone; my name is Ratcydana Kim. I am a health educator for San Diego Family Care. I have been working there for about ten years. I feel like right now where I'm at, it's time for a change. So next, going within the five years to pretty much become better in every aspect. I'm planning to go to school to become a registered nurse. I like health care, and I like helping people."

"Hello, everybody; my name is Tony Laow. To start off, growing up I had a lot of health issues. I was diagnosed with Crohn's disease when I was about sixteen years old. I was kind of at the age where I was ready to go to college and kind of do whatever I wanted to do, but I didn't really have the health to continue through my day or even want to study, so from that point, I kind of decided to take the easy way out. My parents emigrated here from the Middle East, so the typical thing for them to do was to start a business. They didn't have the blessing like I did to go to school or go to college or do what I wanted to do. To carry out my own dream.

"Because of my health condition, I really didn't take advantage of the blessings that I did have. I decided, *Okay, I'm just going to go help my dad in his business, and I'm not going to go to college.* I tried that out for a little bit. I realized, *I'm not really making my life any better; I'm just living every day. Just like, today, wake up, go to work, come back home, go to sleep. I'm making no difference in my life, no difference in anyone else's life. I'm not helping my dad out. He wanted to see me grow as my own individual person.*

"I decided to go get my associate's degree. I went to Palomar Community College for two years and decided, *Okay, I can do it.* I continued, got my bachelor's at Cal State San Marcos in business. Then I started working. I was at Target for a little bit. While I was there, my condition got a little worse. I realized maybe I'm going to go back to school because I was feeling a little better there, so maybe the school was the treatment for now.

"My first class was with Kevin at National University. I decided, *I have a heath condition. I've been in and out of hospitals since I cannot remember when. When I go back and help people that are in my shoes, help them have a better experience when they are in the hospital, help them feel better. A kid does not want to be in the hospital, he wants to be treated like he is in any other place.* I was happy to be there.

"Eventually, I did get a lot better. I picked up healthy habits, healthy eating, healthy exercise. I started a school program that I actually enjoyed, which gave me motivation to continue and grow. It helped me establish my goal for the next five years, which is to continue on with my master's program. To get into a position in health care where I can actually make a difference in other people's lives. To make my family proud. To bring myself into a position that I would respect myself regularly and continue living a healthy lifestyle, kind of just surrounding myself with positive energy and motivation. By taking advantage of the blessings that I do have rather than the ones that I don't."

"My name is Alex. I have known Kevin for more than ten years. That's my brother Jose right there. My goal for the next five years is to complete my bachelor's degree and to get into federal law enforcement, the DEA, or US Marshals."

"My name is William Nguyen. First, I want to thank Kevin for putting this dinner together tonight and everyone who helped put it together. I was so shocked when I came here and saw everybody. I graduated with my master's recently. My goal right now is to work and save some money and open a business five years from now with my wife. I work for the City of San Diego in finance management."

"Hello, everyone; my name is Jose Olivera. I'm from Santa Maria, California. First off, thanks to Kevin for everything. I'm happy to be here. It's great to see everybody. To see a lot of familiar faces and new faces and to know that everybody here has a goal and is doing something with their lives, and is motivated to change their lives around and not just help themselves, but help others in their communities, their families. So actually it's great to be here.

"Currently, I'm a law student at California Western School of Law. I'm starting my third year. In five years, hopefully I can be like Jose and Irving, pass the bar and become an attorney, a defense attorney. I just wanted to share one thing. My sister sent me a picture, and the picture said, 'Be the person you needed when you were a child.' To me, that resonated a lot to me, knowing that growing up, I didn't have a person that I could look up to. A mentor, if you will. Today my goal is to help others who are like me, who come from a community similar to mine, and be that mentor that I needed when I was a child. Thank you."

"Good afternoon, everybody. My name is Jose Orozco; I'm an attorney with the San Diego Public Defender's Office. My goal in the next five years … actually, I'm at a point in my life where I've accomplished the things that I wanted to accomplish when I was younger. I'm an attorney; I'm working in a place where I wanted to work. I'm helping people every single day. I'm in court. I'm arguing cases. It's like living the dream, pretty much.

"But like many here today have said, you get to a point where you don't feel like you're doing enough. You feel like there's more to do than just what you're doing every single day. So that's where I'm at right now. I feel like even though I'm every day in court, helping people out, negotiating the best deals, representing people who are accused of crimes when they're innocent, helping people negotiate the best deals for them, I don't feel like that's enough for me. I feel like there's more to do.

"I believe that we have a broken system, so that's something that I really want to impact. I can't do it by myself, but I know there are people out there who want to do it. I think what I'm saying is, first I need to do my job well, and I need to make those connections, and I need to rise up the ranks in my job so that I can make a better impact in the system.

"So I think that's going to be my goal—I want to place myself in a position where I can impact not just one person, not just one person a day, but the system so that it's a better system for everybody, for the public, for public safety. Also for people who are singled out because of who they hang out with or what they look like. That's going to be my goal."

"Hi, everyone. My name is Owen Orta. Everything for me is brand new. I always kept myself down. I was always smart. I've been in trouble, and I just got tired of trouble. So pretty much I'm just trying to get myself together and make the best at what I can. I learn through other people, and that's what I've used in life. So get myself in the box, and I'm ready to take that step two. What I want to pursue in life. I'm sure of what I want, but I guess at the age of twenty-five, I think I'm ready for it. I've got a decent job, and I'm pretty confident for what I do, and I'm always willing to take chances and risk. I'm excited to be in here, and I'm ready to change. I'm ready to give it 100 percent. That's it. I'm just ready to learn."

"My name is Irving, like Kevin said. I just passed the bar to become an attorney. I think my goal for the next five years … I'm a little crazy in that. I have so many goals; I don't even know which ones to share. I think for one, I obviously I want to start my career. I want to be the best lawyer I can be. I want to start a company. I want to invest in something. In my head, there's so many ideas that I want to do. I think now I have the footing to actually start doing them. I want to write a book by the time I'm thirty. I asked Kevin if he could help me; he said yes, so hopefully he'll help me out with that. There's so many things that I want to do in the next five years, and I think ultimately I can do them. We just need to keep at it and working hard every day."

"I am Agustin Peña, and before I begin, guys, let me reiterate something that's been said. All of what we are talking about would not have been possible without one person, so can you guys join me in a round of applause for Kevin? Having everyone here at the same table from varying degrees of experience … Owen, who is just starting to meet everybody, to Prawit, who's been with the group for over almost two decades, and everybody in between.

"A little bit about me, because some of you guys I'm just starting to meet today. I'm a deputy district attorney here in San Diego, and I'm kind of along the same lines as Jose. I go into court every single day. I'm proud to represent my clients. My client is a different client. I represent the people of California. So I go into court every single day representing my clients. Uphold and advocate for the victims of crimes and do the best that I can. As far as my goal in five years, one of the main goals I had at the onset, when I started law school and when I got into the office, was obviously being a DA—or being a different DA.

"Not too many of us DAs come from City Heights. Who can at least say, 'We grew up there, we know the community'" Who understand the language, the culture, the different people in that community? That's one thing that I bring to the table. My personal experience, which a lot of you all are familiar with because you've been there by my side through them, the senseless murder of my fourteen-year-old brother, Javier, in 2007. I want to be different in the sense that I want to be understanding. I want to be compassionate for both the accused, as well as victims. I also want to make sure that I do my job to the best that I can and advocate for those who are harmed through being victims of crimes.

"In five years, I hope to do that. I hope to bring my perspective to the table. I hope to effectuate some change as well. I mean to, kind of the same thing, keep going up, promote, bring more people in with similar experiences and similar backgrounds, to kind of share their experiences. We need that in every occupation, but definitely in the office. That's kind of where I see myself in five years."

"My name is Miguel Ramirez. Right now I attend the New School of Architecture and Design in downtown San Diego, and I'm also attending San Diego City College. I guess my goal for the next five years is to graduate from the art school and hopefully get into a big graphic design company. My other biggest goal is to push my little brother. He's barely going to start middle school, and I want to push him to whatever he wants to be. I know that he knows that I'm going to do right for him, and I know that he knows I'm also going to be pushing him."

"My name is David Rios, for those of you who don't know me. Five year plan, yeah? There you go. I paint houses for a living right now, but I guess my goal will be try to get a business going and flipping houses. I have a wife and three kids—one girl is nine and two boys. My son, who's about to be eight years old in two months, and my third child is going to be three in September. It's nice to see each and every one of you here."

"My name is Chaz Rosales. A little background on me. I used to work at a movie theater for about six years with no sense of direction at that. I did know that that's not what I wanted to be, so I made a step forward with moving on to something bigger and better for my life. One day I had a class with Kevin. My degree right now is health-care administration. So I spoke with him and decided to step forward going into my career by getting out of my comfort zone. This meant quitting my job at the movie theater after working there for six years and just applying, getting an interview with Tony Laow at Sharp Memorial. Getting my foot in the door in health care.

"As of right now, I recently—just recently—was hired at a medical clinic, which is a good experience for me because I'm new to health care, so I'm using that as a stepping stone. My five-year plan is to graduate with my bachelor's degree in health-care administration. Continue on with a master's degree. Right now I'm contemplating on if I should do organizational leadership, because when I had my orientation with the clinic, I found myself interested in developing the employees into becoming more than what they come in to be. That's my five-year plan—graduate bachelor's, graduate master's, and hopefully do what I love to do, which is help make people better. Thank you."

"Good evening, gentlemen; my name is Miguel Samaniego, and I currently work for Scripps Health. I've known Kevin for a long time. One great experience I learned from Kevin is before I met him, I was always dedicated and motivated. I started a family at a young age. I was always determined to work hard. One of the things that he taught me was not to work harder but to work smarter. Since I've met him, I've been dedicated to go back to school. Now I'm attending Ashford University. I'm considered a second-year student now, pursuing business administration.

"I guess my goal for this next five years is first and foremost my family. Everything I do, I do it for them for motivation. Hopefully, get my bachelor's and move on to my master's, and then we'll see what's in the plan. As far a set goal that I have, I don't have one. I kind of go where God points me, in the direction that He wants me to go. I take life as it comes toward me, and I make the best of it. Once again, I'd like to thank Kevin. Without him, I honestly wouldn't be where I'm at right now."

"My name's Mario Torres. Kevin, thank you. I've known Kevin for about, I would say, about maybe eight years ago when I was going to school for criminal justice and I wanted to get into law enforcement. I work for J.P. Morgan Chase Bank and have been there for about seven years. I've picked up different roles from personal banking to help businesses as a business banker. Right now, I'm basically just getting into management and helping manage the branch. I have been married for about eight years. I have two kids. My daughter just turned seven, and my son is about to turn five years old, five years this coming month. What can I say? My goal for the next five years is to just kind of finish what I started a few years ago before I dropped out of school. I think I had about maybe a semester left to finish my bachelor's degree. That's when I decided to quit because I had too much on my plate with the company and with the new kids, and it was just kind of the cycle of life. You kind of have to say, 'Okay, I've got to do this. I've got to do this.' Also, spending more time with my children, investing in them. I can say I'm really thankful to be here. Last year I went through a major depression where maybe right now I wouldn't have been here with you guys. I'm really excited to be here, and I've now transitioned to go back to work and be with my family. I was hearing Jose and Agustin who were talking about the system, broken system; I went through some experiences where I got really discouraged not only in my career but even with life. Even with this country, where you kind of feel left out. Anyhow, I'm excited Kevin's going to share with us today and Jose, Agustin, and Irving."

"Good evening, everybody; my name is Chit Tway. Today, before I introduce myself, I want to say thank you to Kevin, because he invited me to come here. I live in Utah. He texted and called me and said, 'Do you want to come here?' I was excited, because I used to live in San Diego before. A year ago I moved to Utah, but I always liked San Diego for the weather, which I liked a lot. In Utah, the weather is crazy, which is why I miss San Diego a lot. By the way, Kevin always texts me and encourages me. He's like, 'We've got to keep in touch.' He encouraged me to go to school to do something toward a better life for the future. I want to say thank you very much to him. I came the United State as a refugee because our Karen people were being killed by the communist Burmese Army. PowerMentor has helped many of us, and we are grateful."

"Hello, I am Daniel Vasquez. Right now, I am twenty-six. I have one kid, four years old. I've been married for two years. Right now, I have barely started getting back to get my GED. I have been there for four months. I took my math test, and I passed it. I have four more tests to do so I can get my official GED test, my diploma, and start going to college. My five-year plan is to get to attend San Diego State University. As I am in college, I know my plans will come. I really want to be with my kid, because right now where I work, it is Taco Shop, and I cook all day from three in the afternoon until twelve or one in the morning. In the mornings, I go from eight until twelve or one in the afternoon to school, so I am always doing something. I really have only one or two hours just to be with my kid, and I leave. So hopefully this month or next month my papers will arrive so I can get out and get a better job so I can have more stability and have more time for my wife and son.

"Normally, I don't go to a lot of events that you guys do, but this one, I could not miss. I am really happy to see everyone here still together after so many years. I know a lot of people that are here. The people I don't know, it's nice to meet you and hopefully to see you guys around at more events."

"Jose Morales, United States Marine Corps Sergeant. Where do I start? Heck, I've known Kevin for about eleven years now. When I was fifteen years old, I was a hoodlum, right? He tried to steer me in the right direction and all that stuff. Anyway, I was going through bad times, sometimes good. I dropped out of high school at seventeen years old. I was arrested twice in one month. As I was about to turn eighteen, I was a dropout. I didn't know what to do with my life. So I had to make a change, and I knew I wasn't going to do it alone. So I had to join the military. I went for the US Army, but a Marine Corps recruiter pulled me in. I joined the Marine Corps at the age of nineteen after graduating high school in Somerton, Arizona, where my little brother is at. I was deployed to Iraq, Fallujah, twice in 2008. After getting out, I got a job in 2010 or 2011 with Kevin and Miguel at Scripps. I worked landscaping, and right there was where I realized what I want to do. I followed nurses out there, medical assistants, and doctors, going through their lots. I spoke to them. I asked them how they liked their jobs. I was inspired by their stories, so I decided to give it a try. Went to Concord, became a medical assistant. As I was working as a medical assistant, I really, really loved it. So now I am in Nash University taking my bachelor's in registered nursing. For my five-year plan, I guess the sky's the limit. I am trying to be a nurse practitioner at the end of all of this so I can help out kids in different other countries. The whole Doctors Without Borders—yeah, that's what I want to join. Without Kevin, I probably wouldn't be here."

When Jose finished, I took the stage once again. "I would like to take this opportunity to introduce an amazing individual. We can learn a lot from his life, so please welcome Irving back up here."

"Thank you, Kevin. Once again, I'm back. Again, my name is Irving Pedroza, and I am twenty-six years old with no kids. What Kevin asked me to share with you is an experience that I honestly thought was probably the best thing that ever happened to me. It started out pretty bad.

"I wasn't born here. I came to this country when I was six years old from Mexico, in case you guys couldn't tell. Like a lot of you know, that's not an easy experience, because you come to a different country, and you don't know anybody, and you go to school, you try to assimilate and it's not easy. It's not as easy as a lot of people make it sound. In my own family, I had my own struggles. We were in extreme poverty. I remember there have been many times that we were waiting in line for church fries, getting food. I remember as a kid I hated that. I remember I would talk to my mom and I was like, 'Why are we doing this?' I guess I didn't understand at that time. Now I do obviously.

"Also, as a child, I experienced a lot of domestic violence in my house. So much that I think my mom almost—it was hard for her to survive a couple times. After that, it was the experience I lost my brother to schizophrenia. If you guys don't know what that is, it's a disease that is something that you just go out of your mind. You can't control it; you can't do anything about it. To me, that was the most devastating thing that ever happened. Everything else was there. It was always there in my life. I couldn't change it, but my brother was my one inspiration, my motivation to do things. He was really, really smart. He would have me doing schoolwork; I remember I'd learned long division by the time I was seven. It was because of him. After he got diagnosed with schizophrenia, he was no longer there. I didn't have anybody. I never had a father figure. I just didn't; he wasn't there. So that was tough. You get used to it at some point. You just have to.

"As far as education, to me—it might be a little different than what you guys are accustomed to hearing—but to me, school was easy. School was the easy part. It was like my relief. My one thing where I could be like, 'Okay, I got this.' Everything else in my life was out of my control, but school was in my control, was in my hands. Even then, I had so much stuff going on at home that many times I didn't do my schoolwork. For some reason or another, I was blessed with the ability to still do well. I remember there were several times I had friends who'd tell me, 'Oh, I studied eight hours yesterday for this exam.' My question was, 'We have an exam?' Honestly, usually my grades were straight As or Bs, and the friend who would ask me would get a D or an F. Long story short, education was easy. It was my relief, my one thing that I could control and I could say, 'You know what? I got to continue, and if I continue on this path, I'll be okay.'

"That goes back to my brother. When we were four years old, we were still in Mexico, and he was seven at the time. He told me the only way we could get out of there was through education. It's crazy, and it's crazy to believe, but it's true. I remember him saying that, and I have a really good memory, so I kind of remember that part, and it was my brother telling me that, so it made even more of an impact. Once he couldn't do it, I was it. I had to. It wasn't an option.

"Then I went into law school. Same thing, law school. I kind of breezed through it. I didn't put the effort into it that I should have. It wasn't until like the second or even third year that I started hanging out with Kevin and with Agustin more, and I saw how hard they worked, how intense they worked, how they wanted it. They just wanted it. They wanted to work hard, and they did it. It wasn't an option.

"For example, Agustin—he's very disciplined. If you know him, he's disciplined. And that's something I never had. Maybe it was not having a dad there. Maybe it was me losing my father or my brother. I'm sorry. So it was something I always craved. I never had it, but I always wanted it. I always had the talent. I just never had the discipline. Going into my third year—or it was my last year—I actually graduated, and I was starting to get that work ethic. It was perfect timing too, because I was set to take the bar exam.

"For those of you who don't know, in order to pass this and represent a client and go up to a judge, you have to pass the bar exam. The California bar exam is known as the toughest bar exam in the country. Jose's passed it. Agustin's passed it. The other Jose's going to pass it too. I thought I was ready. I was like, 'You know what? I'm working hard. I got a plan, and with Agustin's help, we developed a plan and I'm set, so this is going to be it.' I remember waking up at four in the morning every day and heading to the gym. I remember I was telling Agustin all the time, and he was like, 'You're crazy, dude.' The gym to me was a relief. Then at six o'clock, I went to the library, stayed there all day until about six o'clock in the evening. Then at that time, I called it a night.

"The whole bar experience—I was loving it, to tell you the truth. Everybody around me was like, 'What are you talking about? How can you love this?' To me, it was like structure—something I've always craved. I had my gym time, and the rest of it was like, for the first time in my life, I was studying—something I've never done. It felt good doing it. I was doing well. I had so many practice exams, and I passed many of them. I passed most of them, I would say. I was doing well. I was like, 'Yeah, this is going to happen.' Sure enough, take the exam—I failed.

"It was the first time in my life I actually tried, and I failed. I remember Kevin and I were both there and a couple of other people— my mom and them were there—and it was shocking. It was like, 'Whoa, what am I going to do now?' I tried. I'm not even joking. I tried. I was like, 'If I can't do this when I try, what makes me think I'm going to be able to do it other times?' Taking the bar exam the first time I think it's easier to study, because everyone in your class is studying at the same time. Everybody's doing it. By the second time, not everybody's doing it, and you're no longer in school. It's definitely a different experience to study. So I was like, 'I don't think I can do this again.' It's in three months. So you had to study for three months. I was like, 'I don't know if I can do this again.' It took me awhile.

"I remember coming up to speak with Kevin that day. I was like, "I don't know if I'm going to do this again.' They just said, 'Relax and think about it,' so I did. After realizing my mistakes, they were simple reading mistakes, which I should have known because I never read. So I wasn't as discouraged as I originally thought. There were simple mistakes here and there that I kind of messed up on. The experience between that time and the time I passed is probably the best thing that ever happened to me. I went from not wanting to do that again, not wanting to take the exam again, to thinking it was the best thing that happened to me.

"During that time, before I passed on the second time, I think I read five books within one month, and that's more than I'd read in my lifetime. I got the opportunity for the first time in my life to reflect on my life, think about everything that I've been through. Think about everything that I wanted to do and where I wanted to be. I read so many things, so many ideas, so many concepts that I would've never thought of if I had passed. If I had just gone through and passed, then I would've continued working and just lived a normal life. I think during that time there's too many concepts and ideas that I read that I could share with you, but I'm going to share two for sure.

"One is, you guys hear from history some of the best successes in the world. They were, at one time, the biggest failures. Abraham Lincoln wasn't considered a success until his fifties. Before his forties, he had failed at everything he had tried. Now he's considered one of the best presidents ever. It's something to fail, but it's another thing to fail and give up. You've got to try. You've got to keep going.

"The other thing is two little words. I have a white board that Agustin gave me in my house with two little words that inspired me throughout the entire time. They are *faith* and *desire*. Both work together. You have the faith that everything happens for a reason, and if you have that faith that everything happens for a reason, then you have that desire to pursue everything that you want. And then, on the other hand, if you have the desire to work hard, you have the faith that all your hard work is going to turn out okay. Those two words—obviously, I knew those words before—but I think from now on in my life, I will always have those words imprinted in my head and always think about faith and desire. Those are two key words that I will always continue.

"That's a little bit of what my story is. I hope you guys take something from it. That is, failure should never be an option. We all come from our own hell, I call it. We have all sorts of experiences that we go through. It may not be as bad as the guy next to you, but it doesn't matter. It's your hell. One thing that you've got to start doing, and you've got tell everybody to do, is to stop using that as an excuse and use it as a reason to succeed. Thank you."

When Irving was done speaking, I thanked him for his presentation and then introduced the next speaker.

"Thanks, Irving, and thank you for all you have been and continue to be for all of us. Every time we have the opportunity to meet up, your insight has always helped me see things differently, and that helped me grow as a leader! Next up, Agustin will share some insight from his journey, and thank you, Agustin. Please come on up."

"Thank you, Kevin. We've had a lot of very interesting things said this evening. Honestly, it's inspirational to hear everybody's stories, everybody's background and different experiences that everybody's lived through. When Kevin asked me to talk, he asked me touch up on a little bit about where I'm at today and my crossroads at this point. Before I do that, I want to talk a little bit about my personal history to kind of give you some context with which everything has come about. It's mostly good that I grew up in City Heights. I want that known for a reason, because there aren't that many success stories that come out of City Heights that grow up out of that community. Especially, like I said earlier, that eventually go into law-enforcement occupations.

"So I grew up in City Heights. I went to high school in Mission Bay. I was bused out. It didn't really keep me out of trouble too much, because I still was really close to my neighborhood high school. My counselor pulled me in one day and was like, 'If you don't straighten up, you're not going to graduate; it's not going to happen.' So I got my stuff together. I made up my credits. I went to night school. I did everything I did, and I passed. I graduated high school on time. That was one of the first times that I realized part of the problem was me not putting in the effort. I could always have done it. I just didn't want to put in the work. I was lazy; I was slacking off doing something with my friends. So I did that—I graduated high school. I started City College, and actually, about ten years ago, when I met Kevin, I was sent to his office at Mission Valley.

"So picture this. He's in a suit like he is now, and he's sitting behind a huge desk, big leather chair, and I walk in. I'm in a T-shirt, some faded jeans, and a black hat, and I smell like French fries from Jack in the Box. So I walk in, and this is a job interview, by the way; he's going to interview me for a job. I was nineteen. I didn't know any better. Wow. I'm pretty sure he gave me that job. The way I was, he gave me that job. Even though I've learned that it wasn't because of what I looked like, but because of what he saw in me, because of the potential he saw, because of what I could do but I wasn't doing at the time—what I could eventually accomplish. That's how I met him. Him and actually Jose, to my right.

"Then they encouraged me to go to college. I thought I had given up. I didn't want to go, but then they kind of pushed me a little bit. I was like, 'Fine, I'll try it.' I started going to City College, and then we had a conversation about, 'Where do you want to be in five years? In ten years?'

"Well, I said, 'You know, it would be kind of cool to be an attorney, but that's not going to happen.' People like me, people from my area, we don't make it to that kind of a position.

"I was the one who was laughing. Kevin and Jose were like, 'Okay, if that's what you want to do, then why don't you go for it?' I looked at them and I'm like. 'Really, you think so?' So I went for it. I went to City College. I studied for the LSAT. I graduated San Diego State. I got into Cal Western. I did all that.

"Along the way, I still kept encountering obstacles. I think one of the biggest life-changing obstacles that I faced was when I was at San Diego State back in 2007, about seven years ago. My brother was shot and killed by gang members. Right there in City Heights, by Cleveland Park. Once that happened, that helped me realize so many things. That opened my eyes to so many obstacles and so many things that come with an event like that happening. That only furthered my pursuit of becoming an attorney and eventually, someday, becoming a DA.

"So I went to Cal Western, and I graduated. I studied for the bar. Kevin can attest to this: I was locked in my room for ten hours a day, twelve hours a day. I mean, I'd come out for breaks and stuff to eat, but I was pretty much studying all day, every single day. I passed. I passed the California bar in July 2012. It is not the same, because it was the first time that I realized, hands down that if you really work for it, you really want something, you desire it, it's going to happen. Along the way, my faith was tested. I was like, 'Man, I'm putting in hours and hours. I put in hundreds of dollars to take this stupid test. What am I going to do if I fail? I can't afford that.' But I kept going. I said, 'Screw it. I'm already into it now. I have to keep going.' So I did. I didn't give up. I passed eventually. I started working for the DA's office in law school, but then after law school, I worked as an attorney. I was kind of on a temporary basis for about a year. They finally brought me on full-time, and here I am—a deputy district attorney for San Diego. That's the mission that Kevin was talking about earlier.

"I have a question, 'Is one's mission really accomplished by this point?' I really don't know that it is. There's a difference between being content and satisfied with where you're at and just being stagnant or lazy and you're not going forward. I have to figure out where I'm at. Am I at a place where I'm like, 'Okay, I'm ready to start doing different things. I'm satisfied; I don't want to keep going forward.' That's a personal decision.

That's why 'Mission Accomplished' is not an answer; it's a question. I don't think that I'm there yet.

"Some of the concerns that I have, and they'll always be with me, are again, I didn't come from a family of attorneys like some of my colleagues may have. Some of my colleagues, I've learned, they come from a lot of money. That's not me, so that to me is kind of intimidating because here they are. They're great attorneys, great advocates, they come from money. Here I am, ton of debt, I came from City Heights. Eight people living in a two-bedroom apartment—I mean, there's a huge difference there.

"The phrase you have heard me use before, 'Dreams and Demons,' is really about your insecurities. There was a quote that reminded me of that bullet point right there, and it said, 'Remember that their dreams are as hungry as your demons. Just make sure you're feeding the right ones.' Don't feed into the insecurities. Don't feed into the doubts. Feed into the dream. The desire. The will. The human will, believe me, can accomplish so much. The human will can do so much even at the darkest of times, when you think or feel that it cannot. Trust me, it will.

"Something else that I want to do is set benchmarks. I want to set goals for myself. While you guys were talking, giving your presentations, I realized what I want to be in five years is one thing. When I want to be a good attorney in the office, I want to be respected, I want to do certain things professionally, but that's only half of it. One of the major things that I want to be, or place that I want to be, in five or more years, depends on you. Let's see what I mean by that.

"I can be the most successful person in the state, in the county, the city. That will not matter if I have not helped you guys get to where you want to be. So where I want to be in five years or ten years is going to depend on whether I've done my job in helping you get to where you want to be. You have all heard this many times; I'm always available as a resource, because I want to help you get to where you want to be and what your goals are. I want to help you meet them. Before I leave you guys, I want to encourage you. Don't compromise yourself. Don't compromise your principles. Don't compromise your goals and morals. Continue to do the right thing. Stay on the right path. Pursue a career. Keep working hard, because it will pay off. I think Irving brought up a good point. Having faith and desire are key. Fundamental. Really important to have those. Before I leave, I want to share a quick story, if you don't mind.

"When Irving was studying the second time, he logged in. You get an ID card, and you get a number and a username to type in to the website and it pops up. The results pop up. We were at his house. It was 5:59. The results come out at 6:00. We're sitting there; we're refreshing the page; finally, the page comes up. We're like, 'Okay, moment of truth.' He's on the computer, he's typing in the numbers, presses enter; his name is not on the pass list. We're like, 'Man, I guess we have to do it again.' It's another three months. Yeah, just like that. We were at that point like, 'Okay, it is what it is.' I didn't want to believe that. I was thinking he worked way too hard to fail again. So I got the card, and I'm just kind of playing with it, trying to compare the numbers to see if they're correct. I turned it over, and I see it says November 2013. I looked at Irving, he looks at it, and we realize that this is the card from last year. So I'm looking at Irving like, 'Dude, where is the card?' Now we're like five minutes into it. We're stressed out. I'm getting stressed out for him. We find the numbers, he goes into his e-mail, he types them in, and boom, there it is. Irving Pedrosa. His name is on the pass list. I'm sure it's one of the happiest moments of his life. One of the happiest moments of my life to watch him achieve that and accomplish that. I shared that with you guys so you don't give up. Keep pursuing your dreams, whatever they are. Keep on going at it. You have people around you. You have tons of people around you to help you accomplish that. With that, I want to thank you, and good luck!"

I thanked Agustin and then introduced Jose Orozco.

"Thank you, Agustin. Your journey has been so amazing, and the things I have learned from you and continue to learn have had so much impact on the person I am today. Thank you. Jose Orozco will now share with us about the journey that he has been on and what happens when you hit a detour not expecting it. Come on up, Jose."

"Thank you, Kevin, and again, I am Jose Orozco, but I am pretty sure I know all of you. This weekend, I finally took the time to organize and clean my garage. It's been packed with boxes of stuff that I didn't even know I had. It was the first time that I got to my garage and tried to organize it and clean it up. As I was cleaning it, I found a report card from sixth grade. Actually, a couple of report cards, one from sixth grade and one from seventh grade. Both report cards were not the best ones. All of them were Fs, a couple of Cs. The C was in physical education. The remarks by the teachers were: 'Needs to turn in assignments, very disruptive in class, too social, a lot of absences.' So that was me back in junior high school. As a result of that, a lot of doors were closed for me—also because of things that I just couldn't control.

"So you've got two things going on: the choices that you make and also things that you can't control in your life. I made choices that closed my doors, but also, on the other hand, I didn't have parents to guide me, to mentor me, to support me, to get those doors open. So my doors, a lot of doors, were closed to me by the time I became eighteen. Another door was closed because I was illegal here. I didn't have any papers. Some of you can relate to that. You can understand that. So nothing is open. You do what you can to get through life. For me, I worked as a landscaper mowing lawns. At some point, I worked at a Jack in the Box with Agustin. Maybe I shouldn't be saying that because he is now a DA—just kidding. My options were limited, basically.

"What do you do when that happens? You get depressed. You see everybody move up; you see everybody move forward—you know, getting better jobs, getting a house, getting a nice car—and you can't because of the choices you made and because of things you can't control. What I always say is at the end of understanding, your own understanding, your own power, comes faith. At the end of knowledge, you start with faith. That's where faith begins.

"It was around that time, I was seventeen years old, when I met Kevin. Kevin was important in my life because he didn't solve any of my problems, but he was the kind of person who encouraged me to look for solutions. So I did, and eventually I was able to get out of those circumstances. I went back to school. I got my GED just like Danny. I went to community college just like most of you. I went to San Diego State University like some of you, and then I went to law school. I dropped out of high school, like some of you. Then I'm here as an attorney for the San Diego Public Defender's office. Before that, through law school, my theme was: one door closes, another one opens.

"When I went back to school, it wasn't that hard for me to catch up, but I took it for granted. I took it for granted in law school. In law school, I tried to make it just like college. I was like, 'Hey, I can do this without studying. No big deal. If you think you're there, review a few things, and I'll be okay.' Well, after the first year in law school, just to put it in perspective, at least in a lot of schools what happens is the first year is the most important year of your education in law school. If you don't make it, you get dropped. That's it. You're done. You don't have that option anymore. So you have to obtain a certain degree of grade, but if you're below that, you're done. In that case, you need a seventy-four or higher, which was extremely competitive because everybody's out there trying to make the top 10 percent. Everybody who makes the top 10 percent gets the best jobs or makes more money, becomes a judge later down the road. Well, with that mind-set, I closed my own doors.

"At the end of the first year, I'm thinking I'll be fine. Guess what. I get a letter saying, 'You need to go see the Dean.' This is the famous letter from Cal Western. Anybody who went to school there knows that a letter from the dean at the end of your first year means you're going to be dropped. So I got a letter from the dean saying I had to go meet with her. I think, *Shoot, I messed up.* So I go and meet with the dean. First of all, I called and asked them, 'What does this mean?' They said, 'Well you're going to be dropped because you didn't pass. You didn't get higher than a seventy-four. You can come back in a year, but that's going to be tough. We don't really take people back. Generally, people don't come back who make it again.'

"So afterward, I go by and meet with the dean, and I'm just not very happy—very depressed because I made the choice not to work hard. I put myself in that position. I'm just blaming myself. I had an opportunity, and I messed up. I'm really angry at myself for not doing well. I go to the dean, and I don't even know what to do at that point. I met with the dean, and she tells me that one of the professors made a mistake in her report, in the grading scale. Because of that mistake, now that it had been corrected, it placed me over the seventy-four. At that point, in front of this older lady, I start crying like a baby—like a baby, seriously. Seriously, like a baby. Bawling like, 'Really? I can't believe it.' Like that, really. That's how bad it was. Then I go talk to the professor who made the mistake, and to be honest, I don't think it was a mistake. I think she just did it because she saw something in me. I made that choice. I closed that door, but then it opened again. I got another opportunity to do it. My second year, I didn't make that mistake again. I worked hard, and I was getting really good grades.

"When I was about to finish law school—at that point, you guys know a few years ago that the economy was the worst. Everything dropped. People were losing their houses. A lot of people were unemployed. People who were graduating when I was graduating were just devastated because there were no jobs for attorneys. Nobody was hiring. It was hard to find a job. Somebody like me who didn't do well in law school because I was not in the top 10 percent, top 15 percent, top 20 percent—I'm not going to tell you what percentage I was, but I was definitely not at the top. Somebody like me would have no priority. No foot in the door with any of the firms or at any of the agencies just because of the grades. They would look at you on paper, and just based on paper, you wouldn't qualify. So I was like, "What am I going to do? I've got a degree, but what am I going to do?

"At that point, there was an opportunity that was open, and I took it. It was exciting, but I was nervous. It was an opportunity to become a principal for a school. I'd never done any education other than being a bad student. I was like, 'What am I going to do being a principal for a school? How am I going to lead a school when I have no experience?' That's one of the things I even questioned myself, 'Am I the right person for this job?' It's a job that everybody—the community, the teachers, the students—are looking to for direction and to make sure things get done. To make sure that kids, your kids, are doing well. So I questioned myself. Anyway, I took the job. After the first year I was there, just to put it into perspective, after each year the schools are given an API score. Each school, if you look it up online, there's an API score. That's how you determine whether the school is doing good and whether the students are learning. Well, most of the schools in City Heights, Logan Heights, or Southeast area are not eight hundred or higher. Most of them are below eight hundred, so if you get an eight hundred API score, that means the school is doing well.

"After the first year I was there, we managed to get the score to an eight hundred. An eight zero six. It was one of the very few schools in the neighborhood that got above eight hundred, which meant we were doing well as a school, which meant I kind of did what I was supposed to do, a little bit. But I might not take all the credit because it was the teachers who were there every day in the class, not me. I just made sure that things got done and the people had what they needed. That's what I did. We were doing well the first year. The second year, it got political. There was a struggle between the board and a few of the teachers, and then the parents got involved. Ultimately, the school closed, and there I was again, thinking, 'What am I going to do?' I thought I was going to be in this position after being there for a few years or a year. I thought that was what I wanted to do then because I really liked it. I liked being part of the community, helping people, seeing kids grow, seeing kids achieve higher education. That's what I thought I wanted to do after experiencing it, but when the school closed, I was like, 'What am I going to do now?'

"The first year I was there as a principal, which was right after law school, I took the bar. I took the bar exam like a few of you guys did. When I was taking the bar, I took it for granted—again. I put myself in that position. I thought, *I have a job. I'm doing okay. I'm a principal administrator.* It was okay even if I didn't pass it, so I didn't put in the time that I was supposed to put in. You get what you put in, so I failed the test. I didn't really mind at all, because I had a job and I was doing okay. But when the school closed, no bar exam, I'm not licensed to practice, and no job, I just have a degree and no experience in practicing anything. So what do I do now? It had already been two years since law school, and everything that I learned in law school was already gone. So no job, nothing. So I say, 'Well, I have to take the bar. That's what I studied for, that's what I went for, and you need to take the bar. That's the only way out.' Just like Irving did, I took the bar for the second time. Except for the second time—I don't know if Irving touched on this, but it's also a mental thing.

"Even though I didn't put in what I was supposed to put in, it's the mental thing. You always second guess yourself, wondering if you're going to pass it the second time. You have that insecurity in your mind every single day. Is this going to be enough? Am I doing enough? Am I doing the right thing? Am I reading the right books? Is this what I'm going to be doing to make sure that I pass this test? Always second guessing yourself. The first time you take it, you don't have that problem, because you don't even know, so you're doing as much as you can. The second time, you already have that knowledge. So you're second guessing every single day whether you're doing enough. I did what I thought was working. Studied just like you guys every day, and I passed and then I was like, 'Well, what do I do now?' So that door opened. Now it gave me options. I can in practice on my own. I can start getting clients or try to work for an agency.

"The reason I went to law school for the many reasons I think are common between all of you guys. That you guys are here because you want to help somebody else. Others. For those of you who have kids, you want to help your kids. For those of you who don't have kids, you want to help others. When you have kids, you're going to find out that is kind of difficult. Regardless, you want to help others; you're here for that, and I think that we all have that in common. That's the reason I wanted to go to law school. That's the reason why I wanted to be an attorney, because I wanted to help others. I figured becoming an attorney would be a way to do that.

"I wanted to be a criminal defense attorney, because in my neighborhood—I grew up in Logan Heights not in City Heights, sorry, I'm from Logan Heights. In my neighborhood, there was a lot of violence. There were drugs. There was everything, but there was also police abuse. There was also discrimination. There was also no representation in apartments. I always heard about reports, how in California our prisons, our jails are overcrowded. I don't think humans are criminals by nature. It doesn't make sense that just because you're in California, there are more criminals in California, that we must be doing something wrong. It's not just that people are criminals. It's just that we are making bad choices, I think. We're not doing what we're supposed to be doing as a society. I figure that by becoming a criminal defense attorney, I could at least help the other side. The prosecutors say, 'Hey, listen, this person, maybe they did something wrong, but he should be given a second chance. Let's not ruin this person's life for the rest of his life.' Just because he committed one thing, let's try to work it out. Let's try to address public safety—your concerns, the victim's concerns—but also let's try to make sure that this person is a productive citizen of society and not hold his hands for the rest of his life. That's why I wanted to be a criminal defense attorney.

"So I contacted an attorney whom I interned with and whom I worked for. He opened the door for me, and I got a job as a public defender. Which as a public defender, that's where I'm working. A lot of it is—this goes back to the thought that your choices are going to close doors, they're going to open doors, but there are also things that you cannot control that will open doors or close doors. That's where the faith comes in. I think, like Irving was talking about, desire and faith. By your desire, you can control your choices, but other things you can't, and I think that's where your faith comes in. I think that's where my doors are that opened; that's where mine came in.

"Before I close, we've been thanking Kevin a lot this evening, and if you think about it, we're all here because of one person—Kevin. Think about how much Kevin has done in this world. Think about all of us. Just because Kevin came into our lives and how much each of you, or each of us, is impacting other people. Our children, our friends, our communities. Now that's just one person. But we shouldn't just rely on Kevin. We should all strive to be like a Kevin. Imagine if we were doing the things that Kevin was doing and impacting every single person around us. Imagine how much we could make an impact on others or in our communities. I'll leave you with that note. I think like Agustin said, I'm here for you guys. If you don't have my number, I'll give it to you. When I talk to younger groups, I always tell them the only thing that's going to stop you from doing what you want to do is yourself. That's it. That's it. You can accomplish a lot by yourself. You can accomplish a lot more with others. You can accomplish a lot more than others with faith. Thank you."

I thanked Jose and began my address to the group. "Thank you, Jose. One great example I have always known Jose for, is when he makes a mistake, rarely does it happen again. He puts controls in place to prevent it from recurring, and that strategy has been very effective for him. I really believe that his detour served many great purposes. He impacted families, and it shaped him into a stronger leader. Jose is directly responsible for pushing me to return to college and earn my bachelor's, master's, and now doctorate, and for that, I am so incredibly grateful.

"I want to talk about strategy for your life. Hopefully, the book *Accelerate* by John Kotter will serve as the framework to some of the things in your lives, as far as what is your road map for the next five years. I'm pretty sure that every single person in here wants to have purpose in his or her life. I know the times that I've talked to many who have successfully accomplished their career goals, and they share that it's not enough to have met their goals. Because then you're thinking 'Now what?' It's having purpose—having purpose in your life and understanding that you're having an impact on other people. It's not how much time that you have in your life; it's what you do with the time that you have. If you fail the bar, you feel like giving up. When you don't get that job you applied for, you feel like giving up, but the bottom line is, understand that the reason that problems happen in our lives is to get our attention. It's to teach us. It's to help us see things with a different perspective.

"So when you look at your road map and you look at your life, you have to first tell yourself that if doors do not open for you, it's because there is something better awaiting you, you're not positioning yourself in the right way, or the timing is not quite right. It's because often, we become our own barriers. You're the one keeping yourself from reaching your goals. Maybe we have positioned ourselves around the wrong people. We have to realize that if we want to make it, and we know many tell us this, we resist hearing it, but that's the reality. When we are at our best, that is what we are capable of. That is why we must treat people as if they were what they ought to be, and we help them to become what they are capable of being.

"Some interesting things have happened that caused me to reflect on my leadership. There's more power in what we don't say, rather than what we do say. I'm starting to learn more and more that the less I say and the more I listen to people and not talk within meetings and instead talk with others more on a one-to-one basis, it is more engaging, more meaningful, more connecting. Oftentimes, instead of offering our opinions, we ought to consider asking the other person if his is interested in hearing it before we engage. There are so many tactics I'm learning now that if I would have learned them long ago, I could have had much more positive impact. That's the natural evolution of a leader. We must be a lifelong learner, a curious observer of our own behavior as well as that of others.

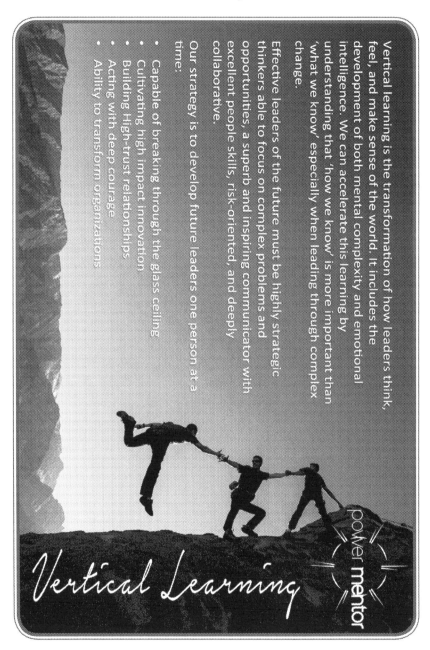

Vertical learning is the transformation of how leaders think, feel, and make sense of the world. It includes the development of both mental complexity and emotional intelligence. We can accelerate this learning by understanding that 'how we know' is more important than 'what we know' especially when leading through complex change.

Effective leaders of the future must be highly strategic thinkers able to focus on complex problems and opportunities, a superb and inspiring communicator with excellent people skills, risk-oriented, and deeply collaborative.

Our strategy is to develop future leaders one person at a time:

- Capable of breaking through the glass ceiling
- Cultivating high impact innovation
- Building High-trust relationships
- Acting with deep courage
- Ability to transform organizations

Vertical Learning

power mentor

"When we talk about leadership strategies, I think we can apply them in every area of our lives. You can apply it to your kids. When your kids rebel, how do you try to motivate them? How do you mentor your kids

142

instead of just disciplining them? What is right with them instead of what is always wrong with them? Right? With your kids, sometimes your propensity is to just tell them, 'No, stop, don't touch that, stop, no.' Instead of considering that it is far more effective to use these opportunities to help them navigate in the right way so they can learn some lessons out of this. Remember, for you to have kids, you're the one who's going to be able to give your kids what you always wished and longed that you would have had but never did—a role model. That's powerful. Raise your hand in this room if you did not have a dad in your life. A role model. Raise your hand. I mean, look at all of the hands. That's a huge thing to be able to provide to your child. In the same way, imagine what you can provide to those who report to you in the workplace. Be the kind of leader you wished you would have had in the past. Bring the best out in those around you instead of focusing on the negative.

"Let's talk about our ability to identify barriers in our lives. First, it is important that we consider that often we look at things through emotion, resulting in distortion. Instead, we should focus using a logical approach in identifying the barriers keeping us from moving forward. For example, in an organization, data is used in decision making. The same can occur in our personal lives. If I keep doing something over and over and I keep failing, insanity is to think that I can keep doing the same things and expect a different outcome. There will be no different outcome. I have to make a choice to change something to get a different outcome.

"Many of you have shared with me that as your lives have transformed and you excel, those close to you, including family, begin to put you down. 'Oh, you think you're all that,' or 'You think you're all that because you're in the Marines.' How many of you have faced that? You have to realize that as you rise up as a leader, the more you will encounter these dilemmas. It has been said that to lead an orchestra, you must turn your back on the crowd. You cannot worry about your critic when you know you are on solid ground and moving forward in your life.

"It is important to align ourselves with the right people to build a coalition, if you will. Recognize the networks you have right here, but you have to understand that no one can open a door for you when you're not willing to walk through it. Before you walk through it, you have to examine yourself and say, 'What can I do to be more effective as a leader?' If you can't say that, there's nothing you're going to be able to do. You will have no chance. So how do you build this coalition around you? You have to actually be able to make people want to help you. For example, Chaz has high likability, and because of that, people what to help and support his efforts. That's just how he carries himself. That's going to carry him in so many ways. If you don't have likability—and I don't mean manipulative likability—as it is said, 'Attitude determines altitude.' You have to realize this whole journey is learning, to help us excel and grow and try to become better and better leaders. Right? You don't just get there; I mean, there's learning all along the way.

"We must set goals by putting them in writing. What is my goal over the next six months? Part of your goal is to put a plan together and say, 'I'm going to do something.' Then you have to start saying, 'Who's for me in this, and who's against me? Who do I need alliance with, and who should I get away from?' Then you reflect, 'In one year, what's my plan? Where am I going to be in one year?' If you don't write this down, the bottom line is, if you're the person who keeps saying, 'I'm going to do this, I'm going to do that,' but you don't do it, it's because you're not writing it down and making sure that you tell other people: 'Here's what my intentions are.' Because when we do that, it does something. That's why companies put mission statements together and their goals and values. It's why the military does what they do. They want everybody to know about it for accountability. So on your first cover inside, you need to develop a personal mission statement for your life: Who are you? What do you want to be known for? What are you all about? And then that's what guides you, so when you go through the tough times, you open that cover up and read it again and say, 'Oops, I'm supposed to be trying to encourage people. Okay. I guess I had better quit being a jerk feeling sorry for myself.' Right?

"Then you have to start checking the goals that you have. Is it realistic? You've got to say: 'Is this a realistic goal for me?'

"Miguel set his sights on completing college. I see Miguel stressing over homework. He's going to work, going home, taking care of the kids, and trying to knock out homework, tons of it. And yet, what is his GPA like? 3.8! He's sending those papers to me to proofread, and I am reading them, thinking, *Wow!* Do you know how much I learn from reading his papers? I'm looking at them saying, *It's unbelievable!* His goals are not only realistic, but he is accomplishing them one class at a time.

"So the potential that everyone in this room has is exponential. But everyone is at a different place in his or her journey. And the magical thing is that in this room, there are people who have been at every level. That doesn't mean that anyone is any better than the others. Everyone has different networks and opportunities to help and partner with each other when we need help.

"What other barriers are out there that we need to talk about? … Ah, procrastination, yes … this is a big one. I can remember a lot of you guys who are here today, you would spend so much time playing computer games. I think it was called *Civilization*. Oh, you guys were going to take over the world. Do you remember? And do you know that these guys would be all together with their computers all networked together like if they were literally command and control for the United States to take over the world? Literally, they were playing this like, they really were. It was unbelievable. I'm sitting there watching this. One of their wives is sick as a dog, and he's just like, 'Just lie down; you're going to be fine.' And these guys one time played, I think, until like, what, five in the morning. Something like that, right? What's funny is I noticed that people will be so loyal to things that are so totally and completely irrelevant in their lives when you can actually really be playing the game of life for real and be out networking and impacting people and doing different things. Instead of it being an afterthought.

"Let me tell you. I read a study that talked about the reason many are drawn into video games. Instead of playing the real game of life, video games mitigate one of our worst fears—our fear of failure. When you fail at the game, you can just turn it off or reset it. When we fail in life, it's hard; it's hard. I remember when Jose took the first bar and failed. I remember being there when Irving failed. It was devastating to watch someone fail at something he had worked so hard for. I mean, it really is. All the things that Irving has learned—those things are invaluable. But that procrastination? I think that's the number one thing that I see; it's probably the number one barrier that compromises most of you. Procrastination.

"It's funny because sometimes I get texts from some of you guys or somebody will say, 'Seriously, how do you do all this stuff? I don't understand.' I'm thinking, *Well, it's easy. You just wake up and do this and do this; it's not an option.* Do you know what I mean? I don't even think about it. Maybe it's because I never got into video games because I wasn't really good at them; I don't know. The reality is that the more purpose you find where you're having impact, the easier it is to play in the real game of life.

"I would venture to say those of you like Miguel, I bet now that you're in college and seeing what you are gaining from it, it's easier to stay up late at night and finish the assignment. Don't forget, almost every failure we have, we're the ones who did it. We're the ones who set ourselves up for failure. So we get mad at the system a lot of times, but the reality is you can't expect justice in a system that's made up of imperfect people. There are no perfect people, and there is no perfect system. But you can control you, and you can control yourself from this day forward. I guarantee you there is somebody who's going to go, 'Oh, Anthony, you know what? They're looking for someone in a law office to help do this. Do you want to work there?' Now Anthony is going to have to realize that if they say, 'Well, it's ten bucks an hour,' he's not really going there for ten bucks. He's going there for what? The connections. Because it's in the industry that he's wanting to get into. Right?

"The other thing is to stay focused on when opportunities present themselves. Do you know what I mean? What other opportunities come up where we can say, 'Oh, you know what? So-and-so is looking for that, or so-and-so is trying to go in that direction.' Or whatever.

"What other barriers are there? Oh yes, for those who are raising their kids and the challenges that come with that. I think that the scariest thing is the reality that those of you who have kids, one day they will be here, and you will not. You'll be gone. And so hopefully when you are gone, you will have taught them so that you will become the legacy they need.

"Imagine some of those stories that I know I shared with you guys and you guys have shared with me about dads bailing and all that kind of devastation. Imagine, on the contrary, imagine your kids telling people, 'Man, my dad was unbelievable. My dad was always there, always standing by me.'

"I look at you, Mario, with your dad and how much he's always been there. Even though your family went through such rocky times. And yet, his dad has always had a heart of gold. That used to always be so awesome for me. Seeing how you guys just were tight, all the time. Always sticking together. Imagine you all as dads having that kind of legacy. Junior looking up to Miguel saying, 'My dad's going to college. I'm going to go to college.'

"That's why it's important when you're going to school. Let your kids see you doing homework too. Because it's important for them to see lifelong learning. For me, now that I'm done with school, a little bit of time has opened up that I'm finding myself reading a lot more.

"Some of us have been preparing for classes and the next step in our lives, and this vertical learning can really help us understand and continually be mindful of our strengths and opportunities. It will help us navigate as to where we are going in our lives. You will know when you start getting on the right track, because all of a sudden doors start opening. Sometimes so many doors, you're just like, 'Whoa.' So this vertical learning is this transformation of how we think. We really have to transform our minds. You can't control or change everybody else. You can only change yourself. That's it. Somebody said that earlier, and that is so true.

"What about emotional intelligence, understanding how we come across to others? You have to try to step out of your comfort zone. If you do a mission statement, for example. If you have a mission statement, you are going to walk in and tell someone straight out, 'You know what my desire is. I want to have an impact on people because I really believe in mentorship,' and on and on, whatever it is. You have to be able to emulate that.

"So that's part of vertical learning, which leads to vertical leadership. We can accelerate this learning by understanding that how we know is more important than what we know. The more education I have, the more I realize what I don't know. In the bachelor's program, I thought I knew everything. I learned the material, and I was like, 'This is great. I know everything. I can solve everything.' In the master's program, I started saying, 'This is really complex. I don't know.' The doctorate is, 'I don't have any idea. I need to research this and allow the data to lead me as a curious learner.' You've got to research everything, and it has to be driven by data. What does the data show? We're emotional beings, and we all will set things up skewed and distorted because that's our human nature from all of our experiences; we see things differently.

"Fact is, leaders for the future must be highly strategic thinkers, able to focus on complex problems and opportunities. A superb and inspiring communicator of excellent people skills, risk oriented, and deeply collaborative. These are the skills that if you don't have them, there's no way you are going to be effective. These are the skills that I know I have to master. Because if I don't, there's no way I can succeed. There's no way. And then I'm learning the more and more I master these things, all of a sudden things just start working out. One of the reasons they start working out is because it's not about me anymore.

"So that's used to develop future leaders one person at a time. Capable of breaking through the glass ceiling. Cultivating high-impact innovation. Forming high-trust relationships. Acting with deep courage. Having the ability to transform organizations. So that's what I want to do at the monthly meetings—to work through this material from Kotter in *Accelerate*. So as we continue throughout the year, let's see where things take each of us on this journey!

"Whatever your accomplishment is or your goals are, they are only as valuable as the struggle that it took you to get there—the tears that you shed and the obstacles that you overcame to get to that point.

"Ask yourself what value do you bring to friendships or the relationship with your significant other? If you add no value or devalue the relationship through negativity or self-centeredness, you must understand that the relationship is destined to fail … You cannot compel a person to continue to endure being devalued through guilt and game playing. So ask yourself what value do you bring to the table? If nothing, you better reevaluate your priorities in your relationships. If you are the one being devalued, you must have the courage to simply tell someone: 'I bring far too much value to this relationship to put up with devaluation games.' Then just move on so people who will value you can have the opportunity to come into your life."

Each of the individuals that have been mentored through our program experience barriers similar to what we have learned through Anthony's story. When we consider the barriers Latino men have faced in their lives, it is really sobering. For example, what are some of the major differences between Latinos and other minority groups in the United States? One of the key distinctions between the African Americans, for example, and the Latino community is this: we tend to lump all Latinos into one homogenous category. It is like saying everyone from Europe is a European. Yet, we all know there is a vast difference culturally between, say, an Italian and a Russian. And so it is with Latinos. A Puerto Rican is culturally different from a Guatemalan or Costa Rican. For one thing, the Central American political system is less stable than, say, the Puerto Ricans who are American citizens.

Then there is the language problem. There are differences between the groups I just mentioned. When you add this barrier to those existing, it can be seen why there is such a wide variance between the two. Of course, there are also immigration issues. Undocumented workers and their families often hide in the shadows and are not anxious to get involved in the American education system, especially when they need financial aid that may be available from the government.

All of these factors, no doubt, contribute to the Latino population having to deal with a steeper high-school dropout rate and a lower college entry rate.

Lack of access to preschool means that many Latinos do not enter formal education until the age of five or six. Nonminority children at age five or six already have one or two years of formal education. A study found that Latino children have only a 67 percent chance of having at least one parent who graduated from high school, while white children have a 95 percent chance of having at least one high-school-educated parent.

Literacy development is another burden for Latino children. It was found that in Los Angeles among children ages two to four, Latino parents were the least likely demographic to read to their children. Children whose parents read to them at least three times a week score higher on state-standardized reading and math exams. Inequalities in household income, parents' education, and child literacy development at an early age influence the achievement gap that continues throughout kindergarten through twelfth-grade schooling.

Teachers and parents lower expectations for Latino students' scholastic success contribute to teachers' beliefs that solving difficulties is the responsibility of a specialist. The term 'barriers to learning and participation' is used. Some studies refer to efforts to shift attention from the student to the context affecting the student's life, which comes from low or no participation and therefore underlearning. Barriers to learning and participation do not supplant the terms *handicapped students* or *special education* with pupils with special education needs.

Learning English is vital for the empowerment and advancement of Latinos living in the United States. Without a foundational knowledge of spoken and written English, Latinos have difficulty with everything from job applications to grocery shopping. Latinos whose families and communities speak primarily or exclusively Spanish or Portuguese must learn English in school. Those who struggle to learn English will struggle with academic achievement.

Race, along with other factors, has had an impact on the education of underrepresented populations. Hispanic students' struggles with educational attainment may stem from characteristics of their culture; for example, the cultural characteristics may include traditional family roles for women and breadwinner roles for men, family loyalty, and financial exigencies. Hispanic women demonstrate higher persistence, transfer, and overall academic success rates than Hispanic men. One reason for this gender disparity might be because women tend to be book smart and risk averse, whereas men tend to be street smart and, perhaps because they mature later than women, less averse to risky behavior. Hispanic men are subject to cultural, financial, educational, familial, social, physiological, and emotional stressors that may hinder their academic achievement.

Gender expectations in general and gender expectations within the Hispanic population in particular may have a negative influence on academic success for men. Despite many Hispanic parents' desires for their children to become educated, the lower socioeconomic stratum of their community perceives it to be more macho for men to do physical labor rather than mental work. A related phenomenon aligned to

Hispanic parents' frequent lack of formal education is the inability of parents, grandparents, or other older family members to fully appreciate the commitment and persistence required to be successful in school. In the absence of strong, positive male role models in the Hispanic community, gang affiliation is the only vehicle for finding and emulating trusted older men.

There are few Hispanic mentors in schools. One possible reason for the shortage is the feminization of teaching at all levels of education. Female teachers, especially in secondary school, tend to be less patient when faced with male student horseplay and tend to punish behaviors that they deem hyperactive or disruptive. A disproportionate number of disciplinary issues affect Hispanic students, especially Hispanic male students. Conversely, male teachers, especially members of the students' own ethnicity, might be better able to channel, and less apt to chastise, the physicality, competitive play, and tactile learning that male students often prefer and female teachers often criticize. In the absence of relatives who have attained college degrees, young men and women require other strong mentors to model college-attending behavior and success. Some researcher noted that Hispanic young men, unlike Hispanic young women, tend to look for and find suitable mentors when they are available.

Another issue that affects gender roles in the Hispanic population is the lack of financial resources. Hispanics are among the poorest of all US residents. Many Hispanic families lack the financial resources to fund a college education. The family orientation of the Hispanic culture places the burden of working to support the family on men, even when they are enrolled in college as full- or part-time students. Hispanic families typically believe that healthy young men should enter the workforce as soon as possible. Some Hispanic men associate work with self-respect and believe that it is in direct conflict with the realities of going to college, causing Hispanic students to feel pulled in different directions. Latinos may want to attend school, and their parents may want them to go to school, but lack of finances, family loyalty, and self-generated feelings of guilt about not working may conspire against that goal. Family or internal pressures to generate income for the household can encourage Hispanic young men to defer college enrollment. Those

Latino students who do choose to pursue a college education will be less able to afford college than their nonminority counterparts and will encounter lower levels of college financial aid. Latino students who seek employment as an alternative to school, especially if they have dropped out of high school, will find poor work availability.

While adolescence is viewed as a key stage for identity development, preadolescents from immigrant families face early exposure to identity issues. Acculturation, the intergenerational process of cultural change that occurs as an individual is exposed to a different culture, has been associated with numerous psychosocial outcomes, resulting in a need for a better understanding of the process of acculturation, how it occurs, and the conditions under which it occurs. Although researchers have examined the context in which immigrant adaptation occurs, none have explicitly explored the effects of context—particularly school context—on individual acculturation.

Students from diverse backgrounds, especially Latino students, bring different experiences to the school environment. In interviews with school administrators, teachers, and other school officials, several challenges of educating English-language learners were highlighted. Many immigrant students arrive with limited schooling; they may be illiterate in their native language, so there is no foundation of education upon which to build. The high rate of transience among immigrant and limited-English-proficient students presents a barrier to instruction. Immigrant students and students with limited English proficiency often enter secondary schools based on the student's age. Limited education and their cultural differences and emotional needs present a barrier to instruction. The influx of immigrant learners and English-language learners contributes to overcrowding in many schools. Finding and providing native-language teachers is difficult when students who speak as many as eighty-eight languages (or more) are represented in some school districts.

Data corroborates previous findings, underscoring the challenges posed by this rapidly growing and diverse student population. Changing demographics in urban and rural settings requires educational professionals to become well versed in the specific cultural, linguistic, and cognitive characteristics of new students from diverse backgrounds.

Educators need to apply this knowledge to ensure the provision of equitable educational opportunities for these students.

Schools attended primarily by Latinos are not on par with schools attended primarily by nonminorities. Inequalities in the level of school access include a high proportion of students attending urban schools that are overcrowded, understaffed, and underfunded. There are fewer high-school courses required for entrance to the University of California and the California State University systems available at these schools. Latino primary and secondary school students have unequal access to college resources and college exposure, fewer well-prepared teachers, fewer experienced teachers, and fewer educational resources. Inequalities in college include a high dropout rate, poor college attendance, less social capital, and unequal access to resources. In sum, Latinos face a multitude of barriers to overcome beginning in preschool and following them through college.

On the Macho Syndrome

Interaction is determined not by a group's defining characteristics or preferences but by the relative size of groups. As group size increases, its members' interactions with members of other groups decreases. Only physical proximity increases the probability of interaction. Members may prefer to interact with other members of their own group. When they are members of a small group, they will interact more with members of larger groups, despite their preferences, simply because their opportunities for in-group interactions are fewer due to their group size. Because the probability for out-group interaction is unequal across groups, the effect of such interaction is greater for the members of the small group.

Some adolescents and young men, regardless of ethnicity, adopt a certain age-related bravado; for Hispanics, this swaggering puffery is heightened by the Latin cultural idea of machismo. For Hispanics raised in the United States, this bravado frequently takes the form of rejection of American goal-oriented ideals, such as educational attainment. Hispanic young men and women feel peer pressure against "acting too white." To ensure that they are not acting too white, Hispanic young men and women may demonstrate resistance to attend school or seem too intellectual; they resist leaving the old neighborhood behind by going to college and moving away. Some suggest that minority youth born in the United States often have less trust in white society and institutions and a less optimistic view of their possibilities to advance than do their parents. For the parents, comparisons with their country of origin, which their children are unable to make if they were born in the United States, lead them to believe that life in the United States is better than it would have been in their country of origin.

One researcher explained that Hispanics in the United States lacked "cultural capital," or the set of "general cultural background, knowledge, disposition, and skills passed from one generation to the next." Hegemonic groups dominate society and education; the art, literature, music, philosophy, and interests of the dominant culture are valued in educational institutions, while these same aspects associated with poor individuals, immigrants, and other nondominant groups are systematically undervalued.

Others noted that Hispanic students join US educational institutions rich in capital that is not appreciated by mainstream culture. Supporters of the cultural deficit theory accept the idea that students exposed to mainstream books, museums, and other societal markers have more of the capital of the dominant culture (the "culture capital"), which is useful for getting into college and graduating, than do students lacking such exposure in their background. Some offered a more nuanced view in which Hispanic young men and women might critique the majority culture and strive to maintain their own cultural uniqueness but not necessarily by sabotaging their own academic advancement. Some have concluded that minority young men and women act out in opposition to the majority culture. Instead, many perceived them as acting in the interests of preserving their own cultural and individual identity along a continuum.

Some researchers cited "noncompliant believers" who associate achievement with the dominant group, although they believe education is the means to success. They reject school and the codes of the majority society. Another identified "cultural mainstreamers" as young people who have a clear sense of who they are but recognize mainstream values and behaviors as normative (rather than "white"). Peers of cultural mainstreamers may characterize them as sellouts or "coconuts," meaning brown on the outside but white on the inside. "Cultural straddlers" comfortably move back and forth between various ethnic groups.

On Integration

Some have argued that a need exists for students to become "cultural navigators," individuals who manage to be upwardly mobile and adept at fitting into mainstream society but still comfortable in their own community and their own skin. High-achieving Hispanic students belong to "dual reference groups," those who identify with the values of both their own ethnic minority and those of the mainstream middle-class majority. No matter where Hispanic students fall on the cultural identification continuum, navigating between expectations at home, in the classroom, and among peers is difficult.

School integration allows individuals to share and learn with their peers and encourages interaction among different people in the school community, which enriches learning. Many approached integration along the lines of scholastic support needs, rather than racial lines, when he stated that children who participate in activities with others learn better because the support of others creates confidence. Others contended this process must be sought in school settings because most social values learned through in-school integration can be extended to life after graduation. School integration is a good start for social integration, because, in school, children learn to respect, work with people who have other characteristics, and live together peaceably with other ethnicities and cultures, all of which lead to changes not only in the way of living with differences but also in the child's ideas about diversity.

To ensure involvement in the process of integration and appreciation of people's differences, there must be a distinction between integration and acceptance. For instance, a researcher cited the common reaction to students with physical disabilities, which is to believe that removal of architectural barriers will allow the integration process to be achieved because the primary role of the school is to promote student learning and create favorable conditions for all. One suggested that mainstream schools must be more extensive in their preparations to meet the educational needs of all populations and to ensure that pupils are exposed to the best general environment. This process requires schools to not only provide access to an established curriculum for the majority but also provide greater equality of opportunities to reduce differences among students.

The notion of an inclusive school environment may involve the development of new curricula, because even though most Latino education reform is being carried out with this perspective in mind, differences still exist between theory and practice. School inclusivity involves more than just changes in curriculum; it requires changes in methodology and organization by which to modify the conditions that exclude some students. Additionally, some have concluded that schools should follow developing changes and continue the process of identifying and overcoming integration issues instead of assuming whether a school environment can be declared inclusive.

Success in moving through the K–12 system and on to a successful college requires learning multiple important lessons, such as maintaining emotional balance, accepting one's biological reality, developing healthy social attitudes, establishing autonomy, and effectively choosing a future occupation and preparation to comply. These behaviors are derived from the development of teenagers' responsibility, conscience, and knowledge of social reality. To ensure that teenagers learn these behaviors, the behaviors must be included in the objectives of K–12 school curricula. Researchers reported that for many high school graduates, "primary schools prepare students' cognitive mind to function in a modern society (read, write and arithmetic and some knowledge of science) and to socialize making them good citizens," while "higher education is mostly professional as it prepares students for work done in the future." The roles of primary education and higher intermediate level education are not well matched. A researcher asserted that high school is a stage on the social scale at which the student is faced with responsibilities, regulations, and authority. The student must respect these standards to be accepted and move forward. After high school, when these standards are no longer in place, students lack the skills to make independent decisions in their own best interests.

Inclusion in postsecondary school leads to problems that differ from those presented in primary school for various reasons. One problem is that students are adolescents, an age at which they may have difficulty relating to their teachers; adolescents tend to confront authority, question adults, and focus their interests on their peer group.

Some determined that postsecondary school tasks are more complex and diverse than those in primary and secondary schools, and success requires students to listen carefully, express themselves in writing, take notes, solve problems, and perform other complex mental tasks. Students must learn these tasks in primary and secondary school if they are to have any hope of succeeding in postsecondary school. In postsecondary school, these complex tasks are carried out in a more competitive environment. K–12 leaders must assess the needs of students' futures and determine instructional weak points to better prepare all students to survive and succeed in postsecondary education. The first stage of postsecondary education for many students is community college.

What value do you bring to friendships or the relationship with your significant other? If you add no value or devalue the relationship through negativity or self-centeredness, you must understand that the relationship is destined to fail. **You cannot compel a person to continue to endure being devalued through guilt and game playing. So ask yourself what value you bring to the table, and if** it's nothing, you'd better reevaluate your priorities in your relationships. If you are the one being devalued, you must have the courage to simply tell someone, "I bring far too much value to this relationship to put up with devaluation games." Then just move on so people who will value you can have the opportunity to come into your life.

"I am so very proud of each and every one of you for your amazing accomplishments and for the goals you have shared for the next few years. We will accomplish great things together as a PowerMentor team! Thank you all for an amazing evening!"

Chapter Eight

Your Future Awaits You

In October 2014, Anthony meets up with me before heading to class. I told him to stop by because I had something very exciting to tell him.

I can't be more proud of the progress that he has made. He's attending San Diego City College and will be transferring to San Diego State University next year. Even better, he aspires to attend law school at California School Law. Anthony is another young man who has beaten the odds and come out on top.

He is following in the footsteps of so many other men before him—Lalo, Jose, and Agustin, just to name a few.

He's made such good friends and works hard on his studies. I can't help but think back to the time when he was that scruffy-looking kid working at a bagel shop. He is nothing like the kid I met. Even though I saw a spark in him, he was leading himself down the wrong path.

Anthony walks into my house with a large backpack strapped to his shoulders. He takes the huge load off of his shoulders and drops it on the floor.

"It's getting heavy, huh?" I ask.

"Never gets any lighter, that's for sure," he jokes back. "What are you working on?"

"Remember on the very first day we met at Starbucks? I told you I was writing a book based on my experiences mentoring? Well, I just put the finishing touches on it. You're the only person I've told so far."

I can't seem to read Anthony's expression. I was hoping he would be a little more excited. He knew his miraculous journey would be highlight in the book.

"Wow, Kevin, that's amazing. I'm really happy for you. I know you've been working really hard on that."

"Thanks, Anthony."

After a silent pause, Anthony finally speaks again. "Kevin, I have a question for you."

"Okay, go ahead," I say.

"When you first told me you were writing this book, you said the ending would be when my felony was cleared. I'm still a convicted felon. What ending are you going to put in your book instead?"

What Anthony doesn't know is that I invited him to meet with me today for a very specific purpose. I have a surprise for him.

"Anthony, remember all along I told you that you were destined for greatness? As you grow and mature, God will clear your felony in His timing?"

"Yes, I remember you saying that."

"Well, Anthony, you have come a long way. You have changed your life in so many ways. You have been excelling in your college studies, and you have been making better decisions. The best part is that your journey is not done. Your future still looks bright, and you have so many more accomplishments to achieve."

By the look on Anthony's face, I can tell that's not the answer he was looking for. I've probably told him this message a thousand times.

"Thanks, Kevin. That really means a lot. You know, if it weren't for you, I'd probably still be selling bagels."

After a quick laugh, I decide it's time to switch the subject. "Anthony, I have to admit there's another reason I wanted you to stop by today."

"Oh yeah? What's that?"

I slip out an envelope that's been lying on the table. "Anthony, here is the court paper I just received in the mail today."

Anthony jumps out of his seat and snatches the envelope out of my hand. He starts to rip the paper out of the envelope. I can't wait for him to read me the news.

"I can't believe it," he says as he scrambles to get the paper free.

"Read it out loud!" I tell him.

He can't help but skim the paper, only reading the best details to me.

"Dear Mr. Anthony … I am pleased to tell you … After reviewing your case … With the evidence available … Talking to the parties involved … Your attorney … I am pleased to inform you that your felony conviction has been expunged!" Anthony yells. "Oh my God, I can't believe it!"

"Believe it, Anthony."

This is what we has been waiting for, and the moment is finally here. We both start to shed tears of happiness and give each other a hug in celebration.

Anthony says, "You always said I could do it as long as I believed in myself to make the change. You were right. Even though I knew I was destined for great things, my record would have always tormented me. I have done so much for myself, and now I have a clear record to prove it."

"You deserve it, Anthony," I say.

"What can I do to repay you?"

That question was simple for me to answer. "Live your life to its fullest, and do for others what we have done for you. Continue to mentor with unconditional love and acceptance."

Now, all I have to do is sit back and wait for God to lead me to another great adventure.

WHILE I MENTORED THEM, THEY MENTORED ME...
ASK ME ABOUT OUR STORY...